"Grace tells compelling stories that captivate the hearts of readers. As she described sleeping on a top bunk of a railcar, I could feel the gentle sway of moving along the track. I experienced desperate depths of despair and immeasurable heights of joy as she introduced me to character after character. All the while, I was being drawn closer to His side and renewing my commitment to His mission. Join Grace on great adventures as she leads you in an unshakable pursuit of God."

—Sandy Wisdom-Martin, executive director,
National Woman's Missionary Union®

"I LOVE, LOVE, LOVE this devotional. Grace Thornton uses personal stories to make Scripture come alive. Her relaxed writing style makes each devotion accessible for new believers, while the depth of the content challenges those further along the faith journey. Grace's passion for making the Bible accessible and applicable to everyone shines through as she embarks with you in an *Unshakable Pursuit*."

—Cynthia White, associate vice president
for student development, Judson College

"Grace's stories are compelling and unforgettable as she weaves scriptural truths in beautiful new patterns. And her ability to take you with her to exotic corners of the globe is remarkable. I am already composing a list of people for whom I want to buy a copy. This is a gift worthy to be shared."

—Rosalie Hall Hunt, former International Mission Board
missionary, author, and speaker. Past national recording
secretary, Woman's Missionary Union®, and member of the
board of the WMU Foundation

"*Unshakable Pursuit* brings Scripture to life! Each page is filled with adventurous stories from Grace's life that astoundingly weave Scripture into everyday life and portray how the Bible changes us. You'll be urged to know and love God's Word, not just for your own sake but also for the sake of those around you and across the world. Read *Unshakable Pursuit* and see the adventure found in relentlessly pursuing the One who first pursued you!"

—Abbey Oxner, former International Mission
Board Journeyman and director of girls'
ministry at Collierville First Baptist Church, Collierville, TN

A 30-DAY DEVOTIONAL

Unshakable
PURSUIT

Chasing the God Who Chases Us

GRACE THORNTON

Blessings as
you chase God!
Grace Thornton

NEW HOPE
PUBLISHERS

An imprint of Iron Stream Media
Birmingham, Alabama

New Hope® Publishers
5184 Caldwell Mill Rd.
St. 204-221
Hoover, AL 35244
NewHopePublishers.com
An imprint of Iron Stream Media

Library of Congress Cataloging-in-Publication Data

Names: Thornton, Grace (Journalist), author.
Title: Unshakable pursuit : chasing the God who chases us : a 30-day devotional /
Grace Thornton.
Description: First [edition]. | Birmingham : New Hope Publishers, 2018.
Identifiers: LCCN 2018007506 | ISBN 9781625915450 (permabind)
Subjects: LCSH: God (Christianity) | Bible. Acts—Criticism, interpretation, etc.
Classification: LCC BT103 .T465 2018 | DDC 242/.2—dc23
LC record available at https://lccn.loc.gov/2018007506

ISBN-13: 978-1-62591-545-0

5 6 7 8 9 — 22 21 20 19 18

For all those who have caught sight of the beauty of Jesus
and invested their lives in making Him known . . .
and for all those who have yet to hear.

Contents

Introduction

When I make this statement, you may disagree with me. But I'm willing to take the chance.

Lebanon has the best food.

Don't get me wrong—there are a lot of worthy contenders. I'd be lying if I said I didn't spend a good bit of my life in search of new and tasty food . . . or just any tasty food. I bet I'm not alone in that. As people, we have some things that are innate to us. One of them is a desire to eat, and eat good things.

Another is a desire to chase, and chase good things.

We can sometimes tame it down with the busyness of life or the inertia of the couch, but we can't keep it down—it bubbles back to the surface even when we wish it wouldn't. We funnel it into bucket lists, and we fan its flame when we skydive or hike to the top of a mountain or pursue someone we love.

But when it comes down to it, that undying spark was put there by an all-powerful God who knew exactly what we want most, even when we don't recognize it ourselves.

Him.

That's what's in these pages: the story of a God who chased us before we breathed our first breath, who loved us before we knew what love was. Search the whole world over, and besides good food, you'll find this—the best stories are the ones of rags-to-riches, of a love that finds the least deserving and sweeps them up in a life they never could've had on their own, a life better than they could ever imagine.

We know it's the best kind of story—we all know that. And the reason we know it, whether we realize it or not, is because *that's our story.*

It's the story we see in Acts 17:16–28, the story we're going to focus on for the next thirty days. It's the story that gives us the unshakable foundation to the chase of our lives, the one that leads us to Him (1 Corinthians 15:58).

He's better than a bucket list. He asks us all to lay down what we want, not because He's unloving but because He's so much better. When we see Him for who He really is, we don't just begrudgingly follow, we run.

We have nothing to lose.

And we have everything to gain.

Day 1
He Sees Us

The big oak tree had split the house in two, and all Evelyn could do was laugh.

She was supposed to sign the papers the day she went to see the damage—the house should've been hers by the time the sun went down.

"But when the storm came through town, that house was the only house that got any damage," she said. "And it wasn't just a little damage—you could actually see the back yard from the front yard through the middle of the house."

And when Evelyn stared through the gaping hole in the house that should've been hers, what she felt washing over her was a completely different feeling from anger or frustration or sadness.

It was peace.

THAT THEY SHOULD SEEK GOD

So often life seems like a big tangle of bright spots, mundane moments, and undesirables—broken dreams, pain, natural disasters, and consequences of our own sin. But often in the moment when God gives us eyes to turn around and see the ways He's used everything to bend our paths toward Him, one of the many emotions we feel is a sense of awe at the intense precision and care of His design.

The day she saw the tree, Evelyn was in the middle of buying the house to move into with her boyfriend. She'd been walking through life up to that point without giving God a lot of thought. She'd grown up in church, and she believed He was real, but she'd never had the scales fall off her eyes so she could see His pursuit of her.

The day the tree fell, the scales fell too.

And she laughed.

"It was like I was relieved, and that surprised me," she said. "I knew it was God."

Evelyn didn't find God that day, but that was the day she started feeling her way toward Him—something Paul said people often do as God bends their path on purpose (Acts 17:26–27). God bent Evelyn's path the day the tree fell, and as she began to see Him more and more, she began to look back and see more and more moments in her life when God had used good and bad to draw her heart toward Him. She let the house and the life there go, and she chose to take a job in a different city. God's pursuit of her only continued all the more.

PAUL'S OAK TREE MOMENT

Paul himself knew what it was like to have something—or, rather, Someone—stop you in your tracks and change your path. He had given a lot of thought to Jesus, but not the good kind. A born-and-bred Jew, Paul had never seen Jesus for who

He really was, and he wanted to shut Him down. The young man had ordered his whole life around silencing people who followed Jesus, arresting and even killing them if necessary.

And then one night when Paul—then known as Saul—was headed to Damascus to persecute more of Jesus' followers, God threw an "oak tree" in his path in the form of a blinding light from heaven (Acts 9:1–19). Paul fell to the ground, and when a voice said to him, "Saul, Saul—why are you persecuting me?" (v. 4) he recognized the voice as the Lord's. And Jesus said to him—*it's Me.*

He soon gave Paul back the physical sight he had lost to the blinding light—and gave him spiritual sight too. But it took three days. Paul waited in Damascus, blind, not eating or drinking, until God sent him a man named Ananias, one of the very people Paul had gone to Damascus to persecute.

Ananias was scared, but God assured him that Paul was His chosen instrument. So Ananias bravely found Paul, laid his hands on him and said, "Brother Saul, the Lord Jesus who appeared to you on the road by which you came has sent me so that you may regain your sight and be filled with the Holy Spirit" (v. 17). Scales fell off Paul's eyes. Immediately he could see.

And God gave him a new life, a new purpose, a new mission.

HE SEES YOU ON THE ROAD BY WHICH YOU CAME

It's no surprise then that one of the things Paul told the crowd gathered in Athens is that God saw them right where they were—that He had been orchestrating the paths of all the nations for all of history so they might feel their way toward Him and find Him.

It was a message close to Paul's heart—he knew the immense value of being seen and drawn and of seeing God for who He really is.

It changed everything for him. It turned his whole world upside down. And he knew it would do the same for anyone else who chose to believe.

It's a message that's been handed down ever since, from generation to generation. It's a beacon of hope for the successful American executive and the refugee fleeing his or her war-torn country. It's a wealth of peace for the stay-at-home mom, the international student, and the Southern farmer. It's the truth that sears the heart of every person who really hears it. *God sees you right where you are.*

And every bit of your life, from small to big, is propelling you toward the place where you seek God and perhaps feel for Him and find Him. Every bend in the road, every hurt, every unexpected struggle, is putty in the hands of a loving and redemptive Father who is setting boundary lines and seasons in your life so you might have the eternal joy of knowing Him—and then meet others who are on the journey toward knowing Him.

He loves you. You're never out of His sight. You never have been. And you aren't right now.

Take a deep breath. Let that truth resound in your heart today. And take a moment to remember the ways He's bent your path in the past so that you might know Him.

AS YOU PRAY

- Ask God to open your eyes even more today to see His love for and pursuit of you.
- Ask Him to show you more of who He is as you read His Word.
- Thank Him for His pursuit of His people to the point of sending Jesus to be our redemption, and thank Him for the specific ways you've seen His hand moving in your life.

Day 2
He Sees Our Religion

Amal was waiting for the last few streaks of pink and light blue to fade from the sky before she ate her burger. And while she waited, she told me she was hoping that, somewhere in the darkness of that night, the god she worshipped was going to show up.

That's what happens here in her city in the summer, when the days are long and the desert is hot and everyone is abstaining from water and food until sundown as part of the monthlong fast. Those who are devout hope that by keeping the rules they will hear a word from the divine between dusk and dawn.

She thought this year might be her year. And as I listened to her hopes, I thought . . . *I hurt for you, my friend.*

I had questions about her religion—lots of them. And Amal, kind and accommodating, was happy to answer. *Do you get super hungry?* It's not too bad, she said—the hunger helps her pray. But as a woman, for one week of the monthlong fast, she is seen as unclean and unable to participate, unable to pray. *How does that work exactly?* She can make the time up later, she said, just as long as she does it before the month of fasting starts again next year. It's like credit applied to her account, and as long as it's done from dawn to dusk, it counts, no matter what day she does it. So later in the year, when the days get dark more quickly, she and the other women in her family will do the make-up week together. They will fast for the shortest possible days, and it will still fit the rules.

As I left her that evening, I rolled that thought around in my head. My friend was so sincere, but it just didn't sit right. Later as my roommates and I were talking about it, one of them put words to the feeling I had in the pit of my stomach. "It's the whole setup, the idea that there are loopholes, that a god can be duped into accepting less—it just seems like it makes him so small."

CHASING ALL THE WRONG THINGS

A small god being worshipped in a big way—Paul knew what that looked like. When he arrived in Athens, he found a landscape littered with little deities. In Acts 17:16, it says "his spirit was provoked within him as he saw that the city was full of idols." It wasn't that he found a faithless city—he found a city chasing sincerely after all the wrong things.

So every day Paul went out and engaged in conversation, told people about Christ, and watched them wrestle with the truth. He talked with the Epicurean philosophers, people who chased modest pleasures in the hopes of finding a tranquil life. He talked with Stoic philosophers, people who believed virtue came from knowledge and who sought to live in harmony with reason (v. 18). He did it all within a stone's throw of the Altar of the Twelve Gods, a site so significant to the people that it was used as the zero point from which distances in the city were calculated. It wasn't a monument—it was an active place of worship, sacrifice, and prayer.

And in the midst of all that, Paul kept talking.

He also talked with local Jews, whose view of the truth was so close to being right, yet so far. They followed God's law just as they always had, but they hadn't yet believed in Jesus as the Son of God, the Messiah whom God had sent to redeem them. As a result, their hearts hadn't been transformed. Darkness persisted.

Paul knew that life. After all, he had been living it until Jesus met him in that bright light on the road to Damascus.

And now here Paul was, watching thousands of people of all stripes walk down the same blind road he had been walking—the one that leads straight to death. The face of Athens was marked significantly by its large, pagan temples. Its altars included one designated to "the unknown god"—Athenians were covering their bases just in case they had missed a deity. Because of that, they were open to new ideas and willing to listen to Paul preach about his "foreign divinities."

He had an audience. He was invited to address the Court of the Areopagus, a long-running group with a lot of influence. He went in appealing to the one thing that anyone could see—their sincerity.

> Men of Athens, I perceive that in every way you are very religious. For as I passed along and observed the objects of your worship, I found also an altar with this inscription, "To the unknown god." What therefore you worship as unknown, this I proclaim to you.
>
> —vv. 22–23

Paul didn't have just another small god for them, one they could appease with their sacrifices or their service. What he had for them was Jesus Christ, a Deity who would totally obliterate the need for any small gods, gods who could be duped, gods who had been contrived by human minds and human hands. He was a God who wanted their hearts for Himself so much that He radically redeemed Paul and sent him to Athens to preach the words that could sear their souls with truth.

In the dark night of their soul, Paul was holding out a message of piercing light—*God is pursuing you.*

IT'S NOT JUST THEM—GOD SEES US TOO

It's a message still ringing out today, seeping into our hearts through the pages of the Bible, calling out to us through the prompting of the Holy Spirit. God's divine rescue of Paul and His mission to Athens weren't something that ended when the pages of Acts ran out. In the years since, God has never stopped chasing His people.

In fact, He's been doing it for all time, from way before Paul. He's been chasing us since before the foundation of the world (Ephesians 1:4), with a plan in place to rescue us through Christ before we had even been broken by sin (Revelation 13:8).

What a remarkable love.

Here in our living rooms, we're in little danger of hinging our hopes and sacrifices on an Altar of the Twelve Gods, but don't let that keep you from letting the light shine into your heart, illuminating the objects of your sincerity. Are there small gods lurking in your heart, in your home, in your desires? Is your most sincere and deepest affection fixed on Christ and Christ alone, not your service or your sacrifice done in His name? Are there things, even good things like marriage or children or family, that crowd out your wholehearted love for Him? Have practices crept into your faith that are more tradition than truth?

In the dead of your night, He wants to meet you with more than a word—He wants to radically alter your heart, to tilt your face toward the light.

He wants to set you free.

AS YOU PRAY

- Ask God to show you the places where your faith may be tainted by the worship of other things. Are there things you love more than God? Do you cling tightly to "the way we've always done it" rather than asking God daily to reveal the truth of who He is straight from His Word?
- Ask Him to reveal blind spots where your view of Him may not line up with the truth of Scripture.
- Ask God to remove the blindness from the eyes of Amal and others all over the world who are sincerely seeking salvation from false religions. Ask Him to soften their hearts to receive the truth of the gospel.

Day 3
He Created Us

"Wow, the glow from that McDonald's, it's radiant. It's almost *ethereal.*"

I can't even remember where that word first entered our day—maybe from the radio. It's not a word I drop in everyday life; to me, it feels a little dramatic in most settings, and whatever I'd overheard that morning had fit the bill for sure. But I'd made the mental note to use it a lot, just to see how many times I could get my friend Caitlin to roll her eyes.

So as we drove across New Mexico and Arizona that day, I applied it liberally—to interstates, truck stops, cheeseburger combos. You'd be amazed at the ethereal glow a white chocolate mocha can have.

Lucky for her, we finally rolled up at our destination—the Grand Canyon.

As we walked around the path of the South Rim, we would stop occasionally, walk to the edge of the rocks, peer into the canyon, and get overwhelmed with its size all over again. We would sit in silence for a bit, just staring at the tiny curves of the river we could see more than a mile below, as well as the dozens of colored rock layers in between. We had done that for a while when we decided to turn around and start heading back the way we came.

As we walked back up the fairly deserted path, we passed a couple of ladies headed the other way. "It's just ethereal, isn't it?" one of them said to the other.

Right there, my day was made.

THAT GNAWING IN OUR SOULS

To be fair, if there ever was a time to drop that word and mean it, it was at the Grand Canyon. There's something about that place that strikes a chord in your soul and screams *other-worldly*. It practically shouts that there's something out there that's bigger. Better. *More powerful than us.*

God Himself put that chord there—the innate sense that we should know the One who made us, the One with the otherworldly power. It's that sensation that drives us to sit on the edge of the Grand Canyon and stare. It makes us want to get to the top of mountains and sit and feel our smallness. It makes us yearn for the divine in spite of ourselves, even when we try our best to deny that gnawing in our soul.

It's that sensation Paul was tapping into when he stood before the crowd of Athenians and said, "What therefore you worship as unknown, this I proclaim to you. The God who made the world and everything in it, being Lord of heaven and earth, does not live in temples made by man, nor is he served by human hands, as though he needed anything, since he himself gives to all mankind life and breath and everything" (Acts 17:23–25).

Paul knew the Athenians had a pull toward the divine—he had seen all their little gods, all their altars. But he also knew that the real God, the One who made the world, needs us to serve Him no more than the Grand Canyon needs a preschooler to show up with a shovel and offer to help make it bigger.

God made everything—that canyon included.

He eclipsed the things they worshipped. He was the authentic in the midst of the counterfeits. He isn't a god of the sea or the sun or fertility like the gods of the Athenians— He's God of all creation. He spoke the world into existence, flung the stars into space with just a word, set the boundaries of the oceans and told the animals where to live. And as Paul said next, "He made from one man every nation of mankind to live on all the face of the earth" (v. 26). God made the first man, Adam, and from him, people multiplied and moved and settled, and thousands of years later, you're sitting right where you are, God's breath in your lungs, His image etched on your soul (Genesis 1:26–27). You're sitting in the world God made, in the body He created for you. And you're sitting in the promise that you can live with Him forever, if you'll just chase Him with everything you have.

How is it that the God who made everything sees us? How is it that the One who knows the stars by name also knows every hair on your head? How is it that He not only knows but also cares, and not only cares but also pursues?

WISDOM MADE FOOLISH

It's an amazing truth, one that got even more real when Jesus came to earth. He was God wrapped in human flesh, and because of that, He could lay down in the stern of a boat on a pillow and go to sleep in the middle of a windstorm—with no fear. Power over His creation was in the palm of His hand. In Mark 4, as the boat tossed, His disciples woke Him up and said, "Teacher, do you not care that we are perishing?" (v. 38). So He got up, "rebuked the wind and said to the sea, 'Peace! Be still!'" (v. 39).

Everything stopped. And when it did, the disciples were filled with even more fear. "Who then is this, that even the wind and the sea obey him?" (v. 41).

Creation had heard the voice of its Creator.

How amazing is it that that same Jesus let nails keep Him on a Cross when He didn't have to stay there, when He could've called for a whole army of angels to rescue Him (Matthew 26:53)? What Paul offered the Athenians wasn't just a superior God—it was a superior love. Paul's God was pure humility and total power intertwined, a mind-blowing concept. To the people who truly heard Paul's message and believed, it was an earth-shattering truth. But for people who clung to the Greek way of life they thought was superior, the idea of a God dying an offensive death on a cross and rising from the dead was laughable. Paul called out to just these types of people in 1 Corinthians 1:20—"Where is the one who is wise? Where is the scribe? Where is the debater of this age? Has God not made foolish the wisdom of the world?"

God, in His mysterious ways, had gone rogue. He wasn't going to save the world through high-level debate—He chose to save it through the "folly" of the Cross, something that would require the prideful "wise" to shed their hard-earned ideas to accept something that made no sense (v. 21). The crucified Christ whom Paul preached was pure foolishness to Greeks—unless they saw and believed. If they did, then they could see that Christ wasn't folly after all—He was "the power of God and the wisdom of God" (v. 24).

God's power. His sacrifice. His otherworldly thoughts that make no sense to us. Folly to some. Others' richest gain.

And Paul said it was for Jews, Greeks—and us.

AS YOU PRAY

- Ask God to help you recognize His power in His creation as you go through your day today.
- Thank Him for His great affection for us in creating us and in sending Jesus to give us hope.
- Ask God to cause the people He created all over the world to think about the grandness of creation, search for the Creator, and believe in the message of Jesus Christ.

Day 4
He Needs Nothing

Snow dusted the ground that morning in Central Asia as we walked down deserted streets looking for people. It had been a hard month for that area—a major earthquake had ripped through the city, toppling concrete buildings and burying people underneath. Lives were in shambles. The pain was palpable. In the days following the quake, we sat in a small room around a potbellied heater with the women of one family as they wept. One of their sons—the father of newborn twins—hadn't made it out of the shop where he was drinking tea when the earthquake hit. As we sat among the grieving, my friend Jenny rocked one of the now fatherless infants, silently praying over him.

And we all wondered—who would bring him the hope his father didn't have?

That solemn thought filled our hearts as we trudged through the eerily quiet morning in the thin blanket of snow. Despite the fact that they were in the midst of a tragedy, that particular day was the sacrifice holiday of the area's main religion, Islam. We had been told that people would be celebrating in the streets starting in the early morning hours, and we wanted to see what that was like. So we got up early to go looking, but so far we hadn't found anything that screamed, "Sacrifices are happening here."

"Keep looking, and see if you find anything," one of my friends said. I squinted down side roads. I didn't really know what "anything" was going to look like. Blood running in the streets? Families gathered around some sort of ornate, golden altar? Dance rituals? I had no idea. Animal sacrifice has always been foreign to me, so antiquated that I might as well have been looking for a woolly mammoth or a fully functional Noah's ark docked in the lake. It was hard for me to imagine how an animal sacrifice might play out in contemporary life.

But for the people here, it made perfect sense. It's a holiday just as organized as Christmas back in the United States. Herds of animals are for sale in the streets, and you just buy your sheep or bull and take it to an easily cleanable location designated for sacrificing—a place like your neighborhood car wash.

That was where we ended up—a car wash where two butchers were white-aproned and ready, hosing off the already clean concrete and arranging different kinds of knives and axes neatly on top of a white tarp. A group of men and young boys stood around talking and joking, their breath visible in the freezing cold. They offered us candy and chocolate bought to celebrate the holiday, a gesture of hospitality.

What is the purpose of today? We asked that question of the men standing around, the ones who had offered us the candy. "We hope that it will appease God and that maybe we won't have any more earthquakes," one of them said.

After a little while, a small pickup truck pulled up with two big rams, feet bound with rope, huddled in the back. The men lifted them out of the bed of the truck and carried them over to the concrete slab. On the butcher's cue, everyone standing around sang "God is the greatest" in the local language, and he put his knife to the sheep's throat.

And the blood that poured out—that was where their hope rested.

REVOLUTIONARY WORDS

Imagine Paul walking up on this scene, where eating candy and slaughtering animals to appease the divine is as commonplace as Christmas, and saying these words—*God doesn't need all this*. That's not far from what happened when he spoke to the men of the Areopagus, translated "hill of Ares," an outcropping of rock that overlooked the city. He said, "The God who made the world and everything in it, being Lord of heaven and earth, does not live in temples made by man, nor is he served by human hands, as though he needed anything, since he himself gives to all mankind life and breath and everything" (Acts 17:24–25). In a city of altars, they were revolutionary words.

They had revolutionized Paul too.

That small statement—He doesn't need anything—attacked the core of what Paul had always believed. That was why he had such violent feelings toward followers of Jesus—they undermined the system he had spent his whole life believing in. Paul was a devout Jew and a student of the law, and according to the law, God did require his service. God was powerful enough to split the Red Sea so His people could walk right through, but still He could be bought with righteous service, Paul believed. And Paul's whole identity was wrapped up in his ability to keep the law and carry out God's orders. In the Jewish system, that also included sacrifice.

And then along came Jesus, saying that the point of the law was to show the depth of our need for His mercy—that we would never be able to keep it well enough to earn favor with God. Paul thought he was doing just fine, and then Jesus challenged everything. The gospel was about what Jesus did, not about what Paul could do. Paul had nothing, and God had everything to offer.

It was a torpedo of a revelation. Paul's all-powerful God could sustain Himself—He didn't need Paul's effort, his temple, or his sacrifice. He had everything He needed.

But He still wanted Paul's heart.

WE DO BECAUSE WE LOVE

To the weak, the gospel brought ultimate hope, but to the seemingly accomplished like Paul, it was maddening. Much like the people of the earthquake town who had been buying animals and dutifully taking them to the car wash each year, Paul felt as though he'd been making significant deposits in a religious account for a long, long time. But the more he recognized Jesus' perfect righteousness, and the more he realized the height of what Jesus had done on the Cross, the more he realized that account would never come close to being big enough.

> **The saying is trustworthy and deserving of full acceptance, that Christ Jesus came into the world to save sinners, of whom I am the foremost. But I received mercy for this reason, that in me, as the foremost, Jesus Christ might display his perfect patience as an example to those who were to believe in him for eternal life.**
>
> **—1 Timothy 1:15–16**

Yes, God delights in the obedience of His children—Paul included. After Jesus wrecked Paul's heart on the road to Damascus, he didn't stop being obedient. Paul waited in Damascus as Jesus instructed him. He went to Athens as the Spirit directed him. But his obedience was coming from a different place—it was coming from a heart wrapped in the grace and mercy of Jesus, a heart that wanted not to earn favor but to please the One he loved.

Do we fight sin? Yes. Do we seek to please God? Absolutely. But we do it with the knowledge that God sought us out in the depths of our weakness, reaching out to rescue us, not because we had anything to offer Him. His chasing us is not out of His need, but His total love.

And our only proper response is to give Him everything we have in obedience.

AS YOU PRAY

- Ask God to show you afresh the depth of your own insufficiency and the overwhelming sufficiency of Jesus Christ, who doesn't need anything but still loves you and wants your heart for Himself.
- Ask Him to show you any places where your obedience might be an attempt to earn righteousness rather than an act of love for God.
- Ask Him to soften the hearts of people all over the world trapped in false religions and religious activities. Ask Him to illuminate the path for them to find the one true God.

Day 5
He Gives Life and Breath and Everything

My friend Susan and I slumped into the seats on the ferry back to England, gingerly taking our bike shoes off. That day, she had talked me into doing an organized bike ride around northern France. Hundreds of cyclists met at the southern coast of England early that morning, and we all took our bikes together onto the ferry, rode the ferry to France, pedaled through the sixty-mile loop, and then took the big boat back home.

I was exhausted. I wouldn't say I had been the most physically prepared for that kind of ride. It was beautiful, though. It had been an amazing day riding through country lanes, rolling hills, and fields dotted with houses and villages. Even though the two countries were only separated by a small channel of water, France and England looked so different in almost every way—the way buildings were designed, the colors of the landscape, the shape of the trees. But one thing in particular stood out to both of us—in the corner of field after field, giant cru-cifixes stood towering over the crops. The first time I saw one, I thought it might be marking a nearby church, but the more we saw, the more I realized it must just be something cultural there. There were so many. It was almost as if they were there to mark our way.

"It was weird, all those crosses, wasn't it?" Susan commented at one point as we sat on the ferry talking about how the day had gone. She'd seen them before too in front of churches in England but never standing alone like that, and never in such mass quantities. As we talked more, she admitted she didn't know much about Jesus past the crucifix itself. The few church settings she had experienced weren't positive, so she hadn't really given it a whole lot of thought. I told her a few stories about Him—how He doesn't like it when church isn't what it's supposed to be either, and how He was passionate enough about that to throw people out of the Temple (Matthew 21:12-17). We talked about His love and compassion for people, all people, like the woman caught in adultery (John 8:1-11).

"I had no idea Jesus was like that," Susan said.

And she had no idea that God was the One sustaining her every breath, even in that exact moment.

IT PACKS A PUNCH

Ever since sin broke the world and broke us, we've been prone to miss the ways that God is sustaining our very life. We miss the fact that all good things come from Him—things we don't deserve, things we think we've earned ourselves. We don't realize that He's keeping our hearts beating even in the moments when we're blatantly breaking His.

That was what Paul told his audience of philosophers that day in Athens, just after he told them that God already had everything He needed. Not only did God not need them for anything, they needed Him for *everything*. "[H]e himself gives to all mankind life and breath and everything" (Acts 17:25). If that sentence was true, it meant Paul's God was giving them breath as they worshipped Athena, Zeus, and other gods through hedonistic festivals. It meant He was holding them up as they did those things even though He was calling them to repent from them or face judgment (v. 30).

For anyone who would really stop and let that thought seep into his or her soul, it's huge—and unsettling. A God who doesn't even need us, loves us enough to sustain us even in our sin and call us to a life of joy—a life bought by the gruesome death of His own Son, Jesus. Our rebellion is a direct assault from our sinful hearts on the heart of who He is. He can't tolerate sin. Why would He want us? His love for defiant humanity has got to be the greatest mystery of all. It's amazing. It's confounding. It's only on the Cross that the tension is resolved, that Jesus became sin for us so we could share in His righteousness. But why God ever chose to sacrifice His Son on our behalf is mind-boggling.

That love—it defies logic. It makes both Athenians and Americans shake their heads.

But to those who choose to follow the road it marks, it's everything.

LOVE MARKS THE WAY

The ferry got Susan and me back to England just as the sun's rays were growing dim, and back home, I looked up the significance of the crucifixes we had ridden by all day long. They're called wayside crosses, placed there to mark the way for pilgrims. They can be wood, stone, or metal, and they line roads, fields, and paths.

They also mark intersections.

That's where the Athenians were that day as Paul told them about the God who gives them life and breath and everything—an intersection. Jesus wasn't just a religious teacher or philosopher like the ones they were used to—He was the Son of God, killed on a Cross and risen from the dead. Some mocked; they couldn't believe He had risen as Paul said, "But others said, 'We will hear you again about this'" (v. 32).

For people who let the message get past their ears, they could tell one thing—it was worth another listen. Because if it was true, everything would be different. If Christ rose from the dead as Paul said, the gods and the other things they had been investing in were irrelevant, to say the least.

God gives life and breath and everything. He topples other gods (1 Kings 18), and He buys us from their bondage at the highest of costs—the blood of Jesus Christ.

And in Christ, we gain everything—a brand-new road to walk, straight into the arms of unshakable love.

AS YOU PRAY

- Ask God to remind you of the ways, small and large, that He sustains you every day. As you think of them, let that lead you to worship Him in gratitude.
- Ask Him to reveal ways that you perhaps live as though you're trying to be self-sufficient. Ask Him to help you cultivate a spirit of gratitude and trust that mirrors the reality that He holds your every breath.
- Ask Him to cause people around the world to think about the mysteries of this life and seek the truth of the One who created them.

Day 6
He Is Not Far

Frank and his small group of friends had been walking for miles with dusty feet, sore backs, and heavy backpacks that were only feeling heavier by the minute. They'd been getting only the tiniest bit of interest in any conversation they'd had that day as they walked village to village in a remote part of Africa, telling people about Jesus in a place where accepting Him can make you a social outcast—or even get you killed.

They thought it might be time to go home.

Almost.

They compared thoughts and tired legs, and all felt compelled to go to that one last house in the distance. And in that compulsion, they trudged on.

As they approached, a man with a wide smile stepped out to meet them. "Come in," he said. "I've fixed you dinner." And as they entered the house, they realized he had a meal prepared and a place set for each one of them. Bewildered, the group sat and started to eat, and as they talked, they began to ask questions about the man's family, including an adolescent boy who was there in the room with them.

The man proudly told them that the boy was his son, Isa. And with that, the group was even more bewildered—"Isa" is the word for "Jesus" in that part of the world. Frank asked the question burning in everyone's mind: "Why did you decide to name him that?"

The man answered, "When he was born years ago, a man in a white robe appeared to me in a dream, and he told me to name the boy Isa."

"Do you know what the name means?" Frank asked.

The man smiled and said, "No, but when I had that dream, the man in my dream told me that one day some people would come and tell me what it means. And then last night, the man in the white robe was in my dream again, and he told me I should cook a meal for you because you were coming today to tell me."

AS CLOSE AS OUR VERY BREATH

When missionaries get together, these are the kinds of stories that get shared around the table—the mind-blowing ways they've seen God rush into their corner of the world in a way humans could have never anticipated or orchestrated. I have a feeling heaven may contain a lot of us praising God eternally for story after story after story of how God showed up in the most desperate, most remote, and most unexpected places to rescue us lovingly and extravagantly, for His glory, for our good, and for the good of others.

We may feel far-flung at times, but He is not far from each one of us (Acts 17:27).

Even as He draws us to reach out for Him and find Him, He's already about as close as He could possibly get, breathing life into our lungs, infusing it into our cells, speaking it into our souls. Paul says it again in Romans 1:20, that these invisible attributes of God—His eternal power and divine nature—have been there for us to see and hear and feel since the world was made. He's the force breathing the universe into life, piling up the waters of the sea and holding everything in the world together. He's the One appearing to people in dreams all over the world, preparing their hearts to hear His name, spurring them to start looking for the blinding light behind the glimmer they've seen.

And He's waiting for them, for all of us, to make that meal and invite Him in so He can be known.

FEELING OUR WAY TOWARD HIM

The truth of God's presence is buried deep in the heart of every human alive, Paul writes. The truth of who God is screams at us through everything around us, but more often than not, that truth gets tragically suppressed or twisted. That's what it was like for the people Paul spoke to in Athens in Acts 17:16–28. They were surrounded by idols to the Greek gods, misguided attempts by the Athenians to credit someone bigger than themselves with the complex mysteries they saw in the world around them.

It's what all humankind is prone to do until the scales fall off of our eyes—we try to find another way to explain the unexplainable, to satiate the insatiable desire to worship something or someone.

It's our broken flesh's knee-jerk reaction to the cry for something bigger in our souls.

I got an email from someone recently who said she had a small group she really liked to go to—she enjoyed their opinions, and she enjoyed their company. But as much as she wanted to, she just couldn't get herself to believe in their God.

"After many years of searching, I still do not know how to know if God is really involved in planning my life," she said, adding that she felt as though her life had turned out the way she'd made it. "I think I want eternal life, and I love the basic Christian philosophy," she said, "but I just cannot find it in my heart of hearts to believe there is a power orchestrating every minute detail of all of our lives."

I stared at the screen for a long time, trying to figure out what to say back. I wished I could show up on her doorstep with the man from the remote village in Africa, the one with the son named Isa, and have him tell her how God had pursued him in the middle of a dry, arid land in a way humans could never explain short of God's hand at work. I wished I could sit down and have coffee with her and tell her stories from my own life and the lives of my friends where God has intervened in ways we couldn't logically explain, friends like Evelyn, who had the tree split her house in two.

But I realized that even though thousands of miles separated me and my friend, God couldn't have been closer—He was right there, giving her every breath she was breathing. He's not far from me, and He's not far from her, and even now she's feeling her way toward Him though she doesn't see Him yet.

And I prayed that He would bring her journey to a crossroads, one where she would see Him for who He is, see the twists in her path for what they are, and fall down in worship of the undeniable Engineer who has been pursuing her all along. I prayed she would soon have eyes to see that He is more than a philosophy to want and her life is more than the decisions she's made.

God is the immeasurable prize at the end of the path.

And once you truly see it, it's the only song your heart knows how to sing.

AS YOU PRAY

- Ask God to open your eyes to see His hand even more in your life, in the minute details and the major events. Thank Him for what He's done. And ask Him to infuse the markers of His faithfulness into your heart and grow that into deeper trust in Him in the present and the future.

- Ask Him to give the people around you eyes to see the truth of who He is.

- Ask Him to continue to draw His people around the world into places where they can hear and have soft hearts to believe.

Day 7
He Bends Our Paths

There in the tent, Maheer raised his shirt and showed them the scars on his abdomen. The marks from the bullets had faded to brown over the years, but the memory of where they had come from hadn't faded at all.

They were a gift from a Syrian soldier's gun when Syrian troops had occupied Lebanon, and if those shots had found their home in slightly different places, they would have killed Maheer. He lived, but the bullets lodged in his flesh brought with them the poison of hate. At the time, the wounds seemed unforgivable. They seemed that way for a while.

But then, decades later, Maheer sat huddled in the tent of a Syrian soldier's family on his side of the border, offering them blankets, diapers, and food. Syria had imploded, and the people who had managed to get out safely did so with little more than the clothes on their backs. They were now refugees, and they had nothing to offer Maheer, not to mention that their people had brought him great pain in the past. But there he sat. "You should be my enemies," Maheer told them. "But I've found hope in Jesus Christ, and I've forgiven the people who wounded me."

He told them he was sorry for the horrific violence that had driven them from their homeland and made them spill over into Lebanon by the tens of thousands. "But even though I'm sorry for what you've been through, I believe one great purpose for why you are here is so you could hear about Jesus."

As he walked from tent to tent that day in Northern Lebanon, he heard story after story of the horrors taking place in Syria. He heard of bombs dropped in their towns, their neighborhoods, their very homes. He heard of loved ones killed on the road to the border. He sat with people as they wept until it seemed they had no tears left.

And he told them of a God who cared so much about their pain that He knew their every tear (Psalm 56:8) and wept with them (John 11:35).

Over the years, Maheer had learned that God had a bigger story at play, one that ends in a homeland that can't be conquered, where no tears exist. While each night spent sitting in a freezing cold tent might seem like forever when they've lost children or homes, in light of eternity, life on this earth fades more quickly than their frosty breath. No matter how bad the pain might seem, if they found Jesus, it would all be worth it, Maheer told them. He knew that meeting Christ would radically alter their lives, that poverty would become riches, that despair would become hope, if they would just let Him enter their hurt and become their whole life. It could happen—Maheer was confident of that.

And he deeply believed that was exactly why they were there.

PAIN WITH A PURPOSE

From the beginning of time, people have been moving across the face of the earth, crossing borders, settling into the pockets of mountain ranges, moving into high-rise buildings in large cities, looking for new opportunities, running from enemies. Paul said in Acts 17 that none of these details has escaped the purposes of God, who "determined allotted periods and the boundaries of their dwelling place, that they should seek God, and perhaps feel their way toward him and find him" (vv. 26–27).

God loves—in an amazing, unexplainable, universe-altering way. And because of that, we move. We change seasons, circumstances, or places, and it inches us closer to Him. Sometimes those time periods are determined by new jobs or a change in family status—something happy. Other times they are a walk through a season of real pain.

But ask anyone who's found Jesus—really found Him— and they will tell you *it was worth it.* I have friends who have gone through some very difficult hardships in their lives, periods nobody would ever choose for themselves or ever want to relive. Both of them have said more than once that if the things they went through were the things that had to happen to bend their path in the direction of Jesus, if they were given the choice to go back and change them, they would live through them all over again.

That's not a normal thing to say.

It doesn't make sense to outsiders' eyes, people who haven't felt their way toward Jesus yet or seen Him for who

He is. How can any path strewn with trauma, loss, heartbreak, loneliness, or grief be the best path? And how can a God who allowed that path to happen just so we could know Him be worth our time? Is that what love looks like?

It is as if we know what Maheer knows—that everything here is a vapor compared to everything that happens after we close our eyes for the very last time. God loves us intensely—now, yes, but with the big picture in mind most of all.

Have you grasped—really, truly grasped—the depth of God's love for you? Not just for humanity but for you personally? It's a love that—even though He doesn't need anything—sought you out for a relationship with Him where He would one day wipe every tear from your eyes and call you His child. It's a love that, with no ulterior motives, died a gruesome death in your place, just so you might live. It's a love that offers us everything, even though we have nothing to offer in return. It's a love that chases us, whether we're in the remote places of Africa or the church pews of America.

It's a love that makes you want to show your bullet scars to your enemies and know that both your path and theirs have been redeemed by a loving Father, if they will just turn to Him too. The very heartbeat of every single person is sustained by Him, even now. But only those who have truly found Him understand that He's worth anything and everything—anything we have to walk through, everything we have to give up.

It makes us see what's still to come as reality and what's here and now as nothing but a mist (James 4:14).

A SONG FOR THE ROAD

The writer of Hebrews talks about that. Over the years, Hebrews 11 has become sort of an anthem for my heart, a refocusing truth for when the things in front of me start to seem bigger than heaven. In it, person after person walked through periods of life that shaped his or her journey toward God. Person after person got to the point where he or she saw God for who He really was and stepped out in faith to follow. And right in the middle, it says these words:

> **These all died in faith, not having received the things promised, but having seen them and greeted them from afar, and having acknowledged that they were strangers and exiles on the earth. . . . They desire a better country, that is, a heavenly one. Therefore God is not ashamed to be called their God, for he has prepared for them a city.**
> **—Hebrews 11:13, 16**

Paul talks about this in 2 Corinthians 5:1–10, where he says our life here is like one lived in a tent, where we're constantly groaning to shake off the temporary and get to our permanent home.

Syrians may feel the weight of their refugee status more tangibly, but all of us who choose to follow Christ recognize that we're just passing through, pitching a tent to get us through this life here, waiting for the day we can feel the permanence of His love in our perfectly healed hearts (Revelation 21:4). God doesn't bend our paths for the sake of the here and now. He bends them for the still yet to come.

And that gives us all the hope we need.

AS YOU PRAY

- Think about the ways God has bent your own path to get you to the point where you reached out for Him. Praise Him today for His loving care of you, even when you couldn't see Him for who He really is.
- Ask God to tune your heart to see Him more and more as the goal of your entire life. Ask Him to set heaven in your heart so that it's the filter through which you see things here.
- Ask God to move those who don't yet know Him into seasons and places where they have soft hearts to hear and accept the gospel.

Day 8
He Is Inescapable

I sat down at the table shivering a little, my jeans soaked from the knee down. In this desert country, where the forecast is "dust" on a regular basis, this was my first time seeing rain.

You'd think it was theirs too. Just as Alabama isn't good at snow, this Middle Eastern country wasn't good at water. A decent-size rain, and water is flowing openly down the street like a river, with no drainage and nowhere to go. I made the mistake of thinking I could make the three-block walk in a pair of canvas shoes and jeans and only be a little damp.

I was wrong.

As my jeans made puddles on the tile in the classroom, my Arab friends walked by and laughed a little—and clicked their tongues, scolding me. But as soon as my teacher Muna closed the door behind her and it was just the two of us, the laughter stopped.

"Did you hear the thunder last night?" she whispered, eyes wide beneath her head covering.

"I did," I said.

"I was so scared," she said. "Were you scared?"

"Not really," I said. "We have thunderstorms all the time where I'm from." I figured she just wasn't used to it, so it made her nervous.

I was wrong.

"Thunder makes me think of God," she said. "It makes me think of judgment. And I'm so scared of judgment."

Muna explained that in her religion, Islam, there's no way to know for sure whether you've done enough good deeds to outweigh your bad. If you've done something bad recently and then you die before you've had a chance to tip the scales the other way, you'll face eternal damnation. That strikes terror in Muna's heart. She can go to the mall, try to fast as she's supposed to, and distract herself with YouTube videos all she wants, but deep at her core, she knows one thing to be true.

She can't forget God, and He won't forget her.

There's no escaping that reality.

WE CAN'T SHAKE HIM

No matter what square foot of the earth we're standing on, whether we're in the aisle of a church or the doorway of a brothel, God is always crowding us, closer than our breath, pressing on our hearts. That's true when we want Him there, but it's also true when we fear Him or try to forget Him. He's so close that even when we try to hide from Him in the proverbial bushes—like Adam and Eve after they sinned in the Garden of Eden—He's right there, seeing, knowing.

We can try our best to shake Him, but we'll never succeed. No matter how far our hearts might push Him away, there will always be a thunderstorm to bring Him back.

It's that reality that Paul was pressing into when he reminded the Athenians that God "is actually not far from each one of us, for 'In him we live and move and have our being'" (Acts 17:27). The verse Paul quoted wasn't from Scripture—it was written by one of the Greeks' own poets, Aratus, in an invocation to Zeus. Though they were misguided in whom they worshipped, the words made a point—even Athenians knew that God was unsettlingly close, sustaining their very life.

They knew it, just as Muna knew it and Paul knew it. But they all had different opinions on how that made them feel. While Paul was grateful no one would ever snatch him from Jesus' hand (John 10:28), Muna would've done anything to avoid finding herself there. Just as the Cross is life to the believer and foolishness to the unbeliever, the idea of an ever-present God draws extreme reactions. To those who don't know Him and don't have any kind of assurance of how He feels about them, it's terrifying that He's always there watching.

But to Christ followers, the idea of an unshakable, ever-present God is everything our souls ever wanted. We can truly rest—rest in the knowledge that He holds our lives, our hearts, our every breath. It means He'll never leave us or forsake us (Deuteronomy 31:6). It means no one can stand against us (Romans 8:31). No one and nothing can touch us. If we live, Christ is with us working out His purposes for our good, and if we die, we're in the presence of the One who loves us the most (Philippians 1:21).

It was this God Paul pointed to and said *this One—this is the God you want. He's worth trading your status and everything else for.*

As I sat there with Muna, I desperately wanted her to know that God loved her and wanted her to be able to sleep through that thunderstorm. He wanted her to be able to rest in the knowledge that He held her future and His mercy sealed her redemption. She wasn't wrong about the fact that there would be a day of judgment—Paul had warned the Athenians of that (Acts 17:31)—and no one would be able to escape God on that day any more than they can escape Him now. But on that day, the Cross would be enough for anyone who had believed in it, lost his or her life in it, and left everything to follow Jesus.

I wanted Muna to see that the unsettled feeling in her soul was telling her she was out of step with the One who created her, but not because she hadn't done enough good. Because Christ was enough good for her.

And I wanted her to follow that unsettled feeling until she found Him. Because even there, even while she sat with her eyes filled with fear, her mind racing, He was there.

He loved her.

And He waited.

THAT LOVE'S FOR YOU TOO

He waits for you too. There in the quiet where you sit now, God is with you. He's always been there. He's never left.

And He never will.

That's probably a truth your soul has long been familiar with, but sometimes life crowds it out. Soak it in for a minute. He's there right now. When that opportunity didn't work out recently, He was there with you. When you lost that person you loved, He was there. The other night when you laid awake, mind full of heavy things, He was there. In everything that happens, every step you take in this broken world, He's right beside you.

And He always will be.

Yours is a God who will never sleep, who will never let you go. He'll be there every step, infusing it with purpose, preparing you for the day you'll walk into eternity, redeemed by Christ's blood, clothed in His righteousness. In this life, there will be suffering—the world is broken, and we follow a Christ who suffered and asks us to walk that same road.

But you will never go it alone.

AS YOU PRAY

- Thank God for creating you with that unsettled feeling in your heart, the one that lets you know there's Someone bigger, that there's more to life than just what's here.
- Ask Him to give you boldness in your relationships with others to talk about that gnawing in their soul.
- Ask Him to increase the unsettled feeling in people all over the world so they won't be able to numb themselves to their heart's biggest question.

Day 9
He Is Our Father

TODAY'S READING:
ACTS 17:28–31

For most of my life, once every few months or so, there's a day when my dad walks through the room, sees me, and does a double take. The corners of his mouth turn up in a grin, and then he'll say the thing he says every time.

"Has anyone ever told you that you look just like your mother?"

And every single time, he's kidding—other than the dark brown eyes I got from Mom, I don't think there's any way I could look more like Dad than I do. We've got the identical nose, for one thing—and I wouldn't call it the subtlest of noses. In the town where he grew up with his ten siblings, people could spot a Thornton by his or her nose.

It's unmistakable. Trust me.

My brother has a lot of Dad's mannerisms, and he got my dad's love for hunting and being outside. My sister got the quiet way he serves in the background, bending over backward to make sure we had what we needed.

He marked us, that's for sure.

That's what fathers have a tendency to do.

MARKED WITH HIS STAMP

That's the image Paul evoked when he spoke to the Athenians—not the Thornton nose specifically, but the idea that family resemblance is a thing. That might seem obvious, but the fact that it *should* be obvious was the crux of Paul's argument. The city's own poets, such as Aratus of Soli, described themselves as children of the divine. "Always we all have need of Zeus," Aratus wrote of the Greek god. "For we are also his offspring."

But with the same mouths that recited those words, the people worshipped man-made idols, calling them their gods. From a logical perspective, this made zero sense to Paul. If they were so confidently calling themselves the offspring of a deity, shouldn't they resemble the deity? And shouldn't the deity resemble them?

Paul knew his audience—a city of deep thinkers. Athens had some of the world's best philosophers, artists, and writers, so he respectfully began his argument there, with their own poetry on the subject. "Being then God's offspring, we ought not to think that the divine being is like gold or silver or stone, an image formed by the art and imagination of man" (Acts 17:29). Instead, he said, we should expect to look like our Father—and we should expect our Father to look a little like us. The two aren't the same—we don't have the creative or sustaining powers or anything else that makes God unique in His position, but we are stamped with His stamp. We are made in His image. He marked us, just as fathers do.

And any Athenians who made that leap of logic with Paul saw their sincere religion disintegrate instantly into flagrant idolatry in the face of the one true God.

The times of ignorance God overlooked, but now he commands all people everywhere to repent, because he has fixed a day on which he will judge the world in righteousness by a man whom he has appointed; and of this he has given assurance to all by raising him from the dead.

—vv. 30–31

A WHOLE NEW SET OF PRIVILEGES

To the Athenians, the idea that they were the offspring of a deity was so commonplace that they maybe hadn't really stopped to consider what that meant.

It's possible we do the same thing.

As Christians, it's not at all a stretch to say we are the offspring of the one true God—and it's not at all abnormal for us to hold this belief from the get go. The Bible is laced with the truths of God as our Father, starting from the very beginning when He created us in His image (Genesis 1:26–27). Jesus also called Him Father from the start (Luke 2:49), and He included us in that picture (Matthew 6:9). Most people who have brushed up against the Bible even a little bit have heard the words, "Our Father, who art in heaven," and maybe even had them tumble from their mouths at a church service, funeral, or even a locker room.

We may know the familiar words of the Lord's Prayer, but do we really know what it means to be marked by God, to be His offspring?

When Aratus made the statement in his poem about Zeus that "we are also his offspring," the rest of the sentence said,

"And he [Zeus] in his kindness unto men giveth favorable signs and wakeneth the people to work, reminding them of livelihood. He tells what time the soil is best for the labour of the ox and for the mattock, and what time the seasons are favorable both for the planting of the trees and for casting all manner of seeds." Aratus was offering them the idea of a father who was a worship-worthy weather vane.

That may have seemed significant to a farming society, but what Paul held out to them was so very different. Not only did he show them a God who created everything and held it together—crops and weather included—he showed them a God who offered them a divine inheritance. If they repented of their idol worship and followed the one true Father, they would gain everything. They would become sons of God. And if they suffered as Christ did, they would become coheirs with Christ (Romans 8:14–17).

Coheirs with the perfect Son of God who loved us and gave Himself up for us—how in the world is that even a thing? How in the world do I, do you, get to live in that reality? The mercies of God are unfathomable. The Athenians weren't being asked to give up their culture and beliefs for another culture and set of beliefs—they were being asked to throw off sin to chase the Father who offered a perfect love and everything that came along with that.

Paul summed it up like this:

Who shall separate us from the love of Christ? Shall tribulation, or distress, or persecution, or famine, or nakedness, or danger, or sword? . . . For I am sure that neither death nor life, nor angels nor rulers, nor

**things present nor things to come, nor powers, nor
height nor depth, nor anything else in all creation,
will be able to separate us from the love of God in
Christ Jesus our Lord**

—Romans 8:35, 38–39

What an inheritance.

There would be suffering—Paul didn't leave that out. To take part in Jesus' reward in the life yet to come, we take part in His suffering here too. Paul had already seen that happen. Before he got to Athens, he had already been beaten, imprisoned, stoned, and pursued by people who wanted him dead. After he left Athens, things wouldn't be better—he'd be shipwrecked, imprisoned, snakebitten, and threatened with his life again.

But still he stood, and still he preached . . . *you're going to want to know this Father.*

AS YOU PRAY

- Praise God for the depths of His love for you.
- Ask Him to show you more of what it looks like to live as a child of the one true God, to share in Christ's sufferings, and to look forward to the reward in heaven.
- Ask Him to open people's eyes to the truth that they have a Creator, One who has marked them with His image and wants to redeem them.

Day 10
He Can Be Found

Somewhere around Christmas 1961, my dad sent my mom a note in the mail with a series of letters written on the envelope—IHAERFY.

It might have seemed weird to anyone else, but over the months before, my mom had received a lot of notes with letters like that—all acronyms for her to decode. My dad was a little bit of a poet, and he loved puzzles. Whether or not he hoped she would figure that last one out, she did.

IHAERFY—"I have an engagement ring for you."

Not too long after that, he made good on that coded message and put a ring on her finger, a white-gold band with a diamond in the center and two on the sides. They married soon after, and she wore that ring for the next fifty-five years.

And then on Valentine's Day 2017, it vanished into thin air.

In the months following, she's torn the house apart looking for it. Every time I visit, at some point, I grab a flashlight and look under a different piece of furniture. I just have to try. And each and every time, as I'm laid out on the floor with my head under a dresser or a couch, she'll walk by and say, "Oh, I've already looked there . . . but keep looking. Maybe you'll find it." She's like the woman who lost the silver coin in Luke 15—she's swept the house diligently.

Except for one major difference—that ring is nowhere to be found.

MYSTERIOUS BUT SURE

It's possible we sometimes see God the same way, as someone elusive who can't be found.

When I first moved to England, I met Nicola, a driving instructor. She taught me how to drive a stick shift and helped me study to pass the UK driving exam. After we got through the first few lessons, our conversations expanded past "Wow, that's terrible steering—your arms are like noodles!" to her dogs, horses, relationships, and a thousand other things.

Then it turned more serious. One day she opened up about the accident that took her brother's life and the way that experience shaped her view of God. "When my brother's accident happened, I prayed and prayed. In different rooms. In different positions," she said. "God didn't save his life, so I thought maybe there wasn't a God."

I sat quiet.

God is mysterious in the way He chooses to respond to pleas for miracles. There are times He chooses those moments to make Himself known; other times His purposes are different, unknown, unsearchable. We see this throughout the Book of Job, the story of a man who has lived his life well and finds himself in the lowest of low places. He asks God for comfort. He asks God for answers. For a long, long time, He gets neither . . . but God has by no means abandoned him.

It's just that only God can see the full story He is writing, with all the details filled in. Only He knows the reasons. Only He knows what we really need and what the overarching story of the world really needs.

I'll always remember a story told by a former missionary to Africa, a man I respect with a very strong faith. Twice while he and his wife lived in Africa, his wife got malaria while pregnant. The baby's life was in the balance both times. Both times, on their way to the hospital in the nearest city, they stayed up all night praying for God to spare their child. The first time, the baby died. The second time, the baby lived. "What was the difference? From our perspective, there was none," the former missionary said. "Only God knew what His purposes were."

We don't always know. We don't always get miracles. Sometimes we do, but sometimes "Thy will be done" is what God wants our hearts to cry out.

He loves us. He doesn't promise us He will do everything we ask of Him, but He does promise that all things work together for the eternal good of those who love Him.

And He promises this—He can be found.

SIMPLE BUT NOT EASY

When Paul tells the philosophers of the Areopagus that God has been bending their paths, he tells them God did it so they could "perhaps feel their way toward him and find him" (Acts 17:27).

God wasn't hiding in the woods, trying to elude them. He was bursting forth in the stars, the sun, and the mountains saying *here I am . . . come find Me.*

He knows our hearts. He hears our prayers. He promises His people early on that they will find Him if they seek Him with their whole heart (Jeremiah 29:13). He told them He would answer if they called (Jeremiah 33:3). And Jesus underlined that "Seek, and you will find; knock, and it will be opened to you" (Matthew 7:7). God would answer in His timing, with His love and His purposes all intertwined in the answer He gives, even if it's not what we think we need. It would be the best thing.

Knock. And keep knocking.

He promises to answer and give us what we need—and what we need most is more of Him.

The problem is . . . we often don't seek Him with our whole heart, with a pure motive to know Him better regardless of the outcome. Just a few verses later in Matthew 7, Jesus tells His listeners to "enter by the narrow gate. For the gate is wide and the way is easy that leads to destruction, and those who enter by it are many. For the gate is narrow and the way is hard that leads to life, and those who find it are few" (vv. 13–14).

It takes totally open hands to walk a road we know will be hard from the onset. God promises He can be found, but the road to Him is a difficult one, and few choose to keep knocking. Few choose to keep walking.

It's simple, but it's not easy. He's able to be found, but the road there costs us everything.

He promises joy, though. Everlasting joy. And He's overjoyed when we run down that road with open arms to accept it.

That woman in the Luke 15 parable? Her delight at finding the silver coin she had lost is a picture of God's joy when one person feels His pursuit of him or her and turns to face Him, empty hands outstretched. "And when she has found it, she calls together her friends and neighbors, saying, 'Rejoice with me, for I have found the coin I had lost.' Just so, I tell you, there is joy before the angels of God over one sinner who repents" (vv. 9–10).

AS YOU PRAY

- Tell God you want to know Him just for the ultimate prize of knowing Him, not for what He can give you. Ask Him to show you more and more of who He is.
- Ask God to call more and more people to chase after Him and to be persistent in "knocking" until they find Him.
- Ask Him to bring people across your path who are looking for God so you can point them to the truth.

Day 11
He Can Be Known

The sand crunched cold against the back of my hand as I lay there in the dark, arms crossed behind my head. My knuckles worked their way into the soft silt soundlessly, my weight making the slightest dent in the massive desert dunes.

I felt so small.

In this huge ocean of desert, all I'd have to do is move, and a whisper would shift a silky wave of sand back over the spot where I'd been. But at that moment, there wasn't even a whisper. The silence was huge as the desert sky forgot the last hints of sunlight and gave over to night. In seconds, it became a rich, black canvas for stars to poke through, white pegs punched in a Lite-Brite. "It almost feels as though you can reach out and touch them, they're so close," said my friend, Elizabeth, who was lying a few feet away. I nodded, even though she couldn't see me.

Moments before, I'd laughed until tears ran into the sand—we were looking at a ridiculous picture where we had posed with a cup of noodles and the camels that brought us out there. I don't think either of us could've felt farther from home than we did in that moment, lying there in the gaping evening shadows of the Central Asian desert, starlight piercing our thoughts.

Still, even here, God sees.

Earlier that morning, we'd taken a tour of an ancient place with art that honored a faith whose followers strive to be like their figurehead—to achieve a state of sleep. Lying there wide-eyed, sleep was the furthest thing from my mind. I sifted sand through my fingertips. "Elizabeth, aren't you glad we don't have to follow something that tells us the best we can do is to one day get to sleep for a few thousand years? Aren't you glad we get to follow the One who made all this?"

Our God is bigger than the sky, yet He sees us. He doesn't need anything or any human hands to serve Him, yet He loves us and pursues us so we can spend eternity reigning with Him.

The silence reigned a little while longer, and then we found ourselves singing. I thrust my palms into the night sky, praising the One whose love comes to find us, no matter what square foot of earth we are standing on, no matter how remote or how normal.

He reaches for us. We just have to reach back.

LIFE OFFERED IN OUTSTRETCHED HANDS

When Paul had his oak tree moment on the road to Damascus (Acts 9), one thing became abundantly clear to him—Jesus was who He said He was. And that meant everything Jesus had said about Himself was suddenly all true. It meant He was the Way, the Truth, and the Life, and that without Jesus, Paul's religion wasn't enough to get him to the Father

(John 14:6). It meant that Jesus' triumph over sin and death in His Crucifixion and Resurrection was real. It meant the life He promised was a real offer to all who would believe, turn from their sin, and love Him above everyone and everything else.

It's a big ask when you look at it from ground level. But from Jesus' perspective, you lose little and gain everything.

A friend of mine—an intellectual guy with a doctorate from a prestigious school—likes to wrestle with tough questions about creation and other scientific topics. He didn't grow up in church but had come to faith in college, which honestly surprised me, given all his unresolved questions. One day I finally asked him what had made him decide to believe even though he hadn't yet found all the answers he wanted. His response? Not only had he experienced Jesus himself, but also there was plenty of reliable, historical proof that Jesus had walked the earth just as He said. And even past that, hundreds of people who had truly known Him had been changed so radically that they were willing to die for Him—people like those Paul had persecuted. They had seen Jesus for who He was, and that was more than enough for them.

It was more than enough for my friend too.

Because in Jesus, they found more than empty promises, more than fear of possible judgment, more than the hope of an eternal state of sleep. They found radical hope. Love. Joy. They found an offer of eternity spent face to face with Him.

And it was worth their whole life.

That's what happens when we see the hand outstretched toward us and recognize the heart of the One who's extending it—we lay everything down to chase Him. Long after the blinding light of recognition has faded, we still have its impression seared in our souls, reminding us who we belong to and why we follow Him. Like Paul and all those who came before us, we throw off the weight that so easily entangles, and we run as fast as we can toward Him, His light tucked in our hearts and guiding us home (Hebrews 12:1–2).

And little by little, the things of this world begin to fade away.

WE REACH BACK

There in the desert, starlight traced the edges of my outstretched hands. It's a moment I'll never forget.

But the next morning, as I drank instant coffee from a paper cup and watched the sun pierce the sky over the dunes, the thought that warmed me wasn't so much that this was a once-in-a-lifetime kind of moment. It was the thought that these moments—moments when I feel His grandness bursting my heart—pierce my every day. In my car. At my desk. When I run, when I fold laundry, when I get up early to read the Bible. His love finds me. His light stays with me, and I remember what I've seen. He's there with me, sustaining my every breath, reminding me of who He is.

Sometimes when we find ourselves on a mountaintop, we feel as though our heart is quickened to realize His presence. And in some ways it is—by design. But those moments were never meant for us to walk away and forget who He is. We pack that mountain, that sunrise, that starry night into our hearts and they gather together in collective praise every time we feel Him in our quiet cup of coffee, every time we talk to Him while we fold clothes, every time we do our job as an act of worship to Him. We soak our hearts in the truth of who He is, truth laced through the pages of His Word, truth He uses to chase us down and set us free.

Wherever we are, His love pursues us. And we can stretch our hands toward Him from right where we are and say *yes, please—more of that.*

AS YOU PRAY

- Ask God to make Himself known to you in new ways today through the truth of His Word so that you can know Him for who He really is—the prize worth your whole life.
- Ask Him to give you strength to lay down the things you might be holding onto so you can chase Him with nothing holding you back.
- Ask Him to reveal Himself to the people around you who haven't yet seen Him for who He is.

Day 12
His Love Is Personal

My hands shook as I tore open the letter.

I'd graduated from college a few weeks before, and I was back at my parents' house in Mississippi, unemployed and ready to bust out of the cocoon. Just before school ended, I'd interviewed for a job I really wanted, and in the end, the woman doing the interview had shaken my hand and said they would save me a desk. I was beyond excited. All we were waiting on was the paperwork to go through and for me to get my degree in hand.

And several weeks later, the more I drummed my fingers on the table, the more nervous I got.

At that point, technologically speaking, the world was a bit like me—just starting to bust out of its cocoon and stretch its legs. I got my first nonemergency cell phone the summer after my sophomore year, a brick of a phone with a change-able faceplate. (I got a red sparkly one, just in case you were curious.) When it came to the Internet, we had it, but I was still stretching a dial-up phone cord down the hall so I could use my laptop on the couch. And when it came to getting a new job, I had been waiting on that snail-mail letter. It had been like waiting for paint to dry.

And now it was time. I took the letter out and, with trembling hands, read its message.

The job wasn't mine anymore.

There had been a budget crunch and a hiring freeze, all within the few weeks since we shook hands on the job. I'd turned down other things, putting all my eggs in that basket, and now all the doors were shut.

I blinked back tears, opened up my massively heavy laptop, hit "dial up," and started emailing anyone and everyone I could think of who might be able to give me some work, any kind, anywhere.

I didn't know it at the time, but God was massively bending my path, funneling me straight into Birmingham, Alabama—the place that would become my Athens.

LESS ABOUT ESCAPE, MORE ABOUT LOVE

I still remember it, the moment I could look back over my shoulder and see God's intensely personal pursuit of me and how it stretched across my entire life. He had been speaking it to me through my parents, through mentors in college, and through pastors. He had been gently calling my heart to wake up, even as I chased relationships and jobs and saw my plans fall apart and dreams fail.

And He had been using it all to guide me to a place where I might see Him for who He really is.

Up until then, I'd respected God and wanted to please Him. I would've said I loved Him, even that I wanted to do missions one day, but in hindsight, the sentiment was much more reverence than love. It was more about who I thought He expected me to be and what I thought He expected me to do, and a lot less about knowing Him for who He really is.

But one day, at the end of myself, He made Himself known. He used slammed doors and painful seasons, difficult questions, and lost relationships to drive me to that point, but He also used people who walked into the wasteland of my idols at just the right time and spoke truth—*God is love. He's everything. And He's worth giving up everything to love.*

You've always thought you wanted God, but what you really wanted was the life you thought God would give you here on earth. He owes you nothing, but He offers you everything—in Himself. He is your whole life.

And the love of God starts by knowing the truth about who He is—by reading His Word.

I felt like the philosophers who talked with Paul and then took him to speak to the rest of the Areopagus—"May we know what this new teaching is that you are presenting? For you bring some strange things to our ears. We wish to know therefore what these things mean" (Acts 17:19–20).

For years, I'd tried to read the Bible off and on, but I'd been reading it at random—whatever passage a devotional highlighted or wherever I happened to open up to that day. But all of a sudden, after a season of pain when things didn't make sense, my pastor in Birmingham spoke the words, and it was as though I was hearing them for the first time: *The Bible is one big story of redemption, starting with how God created it to be, then we broke it with our rebellion, and everything after that is a quest for Him to win us back so we can love and worship Him.*

Then one day He's going to set everything right again, and we'll get to be with Him forever. It's not that we please God and escape hell—it's that we chase God and then get to spend eternity with the One we love.

Once that story caught hold in my heart, it was as though the whole Bible lit up. God began to jump off the pages. Chapters and passages began to make sense in the context of the big story, not just as individual stories or verses that I was trying to make fit my life. The verses I'd learned as a child sprang to life in my heart, finding their place in the overarching narrative. It was as though I had a new pair of eyes, a new heart.

A new Love to pursue.

HE'S PURSUING YOU

Have you gotten to the point where you can feel the momentum of God's story in your life, spurring you to chase after Him, pressing you to want to know Him better? Do you long for the culmination of His story in heaven?

It's the story that captured Maheer, the one he wanted to take to the Syrian refugees. It's the story Isa's father became a part of when he welcomed the small band of believers into his home in Africa and let them share hope with him. It screams of a God who goes to great lengths to find us, who longs to redeem us if we'll just hold our whole hearts out to Him with open hands.

It's a story laced with love—deep, personal love. And it's pursuing you even now.

AS YOU PRAY

- Ask God to open your eyes to the depths of His love for you, love that's pursuing you personally.
- Ask Him to show you who He really is through the pages of His Word. If this area feels like a struggle, consider reaching out to someone who could mentor you in how to read it in a way that stays true to the meaning God intended to infuse in its pages.
- Ask Him to put people in your path you could disciple and meet with regularly to help them know how to study the Bible. We learn for ourselves, but we also learn so we can pass it on!

Day 13
We Trust Him with Everything

I sat on the couch in the quiet, picking at the small, threadbare spot in the blue slipcover. Frayed, I thought. I'm frayed. And a little afraid.

It's not often we let ourselves go into the space where we're silent and vulnerable with our deepest fears, deepest desires, deepest hurts. It's even more rare when we put ourselves in that space on purpose. Maybe it's because we're afraid to fully see our frayedness. Maybe it's just plain easier to be distracted. Or maybe it's because we're scared that when we finally sit still and put it all out there, God won't show up. And if we lay it all out, and He doesn't show up to rush into that space, will our emotions overwhelm us?

Discomfort is a feeling we don't really love. But rawness and rejection are feelings we avoid at pretty much any cost.

I recently got to meet a new friend who's been walking some hard roads. We talked for a few minutes here and there before she sat down beside me at one point and said quietly, "I really want it. I know God's there. But I just can't seem to get it."

The "it" was peace. But she was afraid if she sat still, unbearable emptiness would gnaw at her frayed soul rather than peace rushing in and putting it back together. It's a valid fear. I don't know that most of us haven't felt that way before. Because what if it takes more than once? What if the first time we open our souls to the silence, it feels like salt in our wounds? What if it still does the second time? And the third time?

But what if, in order to really know God, that's what we have to do? What if we have to face ourselves honestly and devote time to tune our hearts to want God more than anything else? What if we have to be willing to keep stepping into that silent space and tell Him we're ready and willing to lay down the things we want—all of them—if we can get all of Him in return? And if the cost is a little discomfort, we still want Him. And if the cost is all of ourselves, if it's anything and everything, we still want Him.

It's not easy. But it's worth it.

JOY THAT OVERSHADOWS OUR PAIN

That's what Jesus asked of us—willingness to walk into the discomfort of offering up everything we have, everything we feel, everything we want, and everything we are. In Luke 9:23–24, He told the crowds, "If anyone would come after me, let him deny himself and take up his cross daily and follow me. For whoever would save his life will lose it, but whoever loses his life for my sake will save it." A little later, when someone said to Him, "I will follow you wherever you go," He told him that foxes have holes and birds have nests, but He has nowhere to call home (vv. 57–58). He told another that he had to be willing to leave his family behind, to start a new life of all-out commitment and not look back (v. 62).

That wasn't the only place He used that kind of language. In Matthew 10:37–38, He said, "Whoever loves father or mother more than me is not worthy of me, and whoever loves son or daughter more than me is not worthy of me."

That's the choice Paul faced when Jesus met him on the road to Damascus and told Paul He had a different path for him to follow. It would be one that required a lot of sacrifice. But Paul knew that if Jesus was who He said He was, it would be worth it, no matter what. Paul later said, "I have learned in whatever situation I am to be content. I know how to be brought low, and I know how to abound. In any and every circumstance, I have learned the secret of facing plenty and hunger, abundance and need. I can do all things through him who strengthens me" (Philippians 4:11–13).

There may be loss or pain if you follow Jesus. The path of your life may not look like what you thought it was supposed to look like. You may be asked to give up things you wanted or to walk through seasons you never wanted to walk through. But the baseline is this: when we lose our life for the sake of Christ, we find it (Matthew 10:39). And we find that it's far, far better.

He promised His disciples time and time again that any pain would pale in comparison to the joy that awaits—perfect, real, eternal joy.

It's Real, and It Can Be Had

As I sat beside my friend, all I could think to say back was . . . that peace you're looking for in Jesus, it's real. It's real, and it's worth it. Because sometimes when you're in that place where the salt rubs, where the ache is real, where numbness seems like a better option, "It'll get better" isn't what you need to hear. "Hang in there" doesn't provide comfort.

Sometimes more than you need to *hear* anything you need to *see* something—and that something is what real peace and contentment from Jesus looks like when it's splashed across someone's face, across someone's life.

I remember being in that place where silence meant salt rubbing. The only thing that made me sit still, read the Bible, and keep asking God to show me who He really was at any cost was that I saw some people who really loved Jesus—people who wore it a lot differently from the way I did. I didn't know how to get it. I didn't know what it would feel like. But I knew it had to be different, or they wouldn't be so different. I knew it had to be real.

And that meant I could have it too.

I just had to lean in, even if it hurt, even if it felt dry.

I was driving somewhere recently with a friend, and we talked about how easy it is for us to distract ourselves and not ever sit still, even when we know doing it is worth it. And she said, "It's such a hard thing to make ourselves do sometimes, especially when we're not in the habit. But it really does make such a difference. And if you think about it, God is smart in the way He rigged this. Good things always take work and sacrifice, so why should the best thing we can have not take everything we have?"

She's right. It's real, but it's not easy. It's free, but it costs everything. It starts in the quiet of our hearts with the whisper of His truth—the silence of our surrender, then the roar of His peace.

He'll show up. He always does—when we give it everything we have. "You will seek me and find me, when you seek me with all your heart" (Jeremiah 29:13).

AS YOU PRAY

- Ask God to invade your space—to point out the parts of your heart you're hanging onto, just as He did for those who said they wanted to follow Him at the end of Luke 9.
- Ask Him to fill you up with Himself and with the peace that comes only from knowing and following Him.
- Ask Him to help you lean in, keep reading and keep offering Him the vulnerable places of your heart.

Day 14
We Thirst for Him

TODAY'S READING:
ACTS 17:16–28

The waist-deep water was clear to my toes, and I felt its cool current cut clear to my soul. *How do I get more of this in my life?*

That week in the Middle East, the sun had baked our building like a piece of baklava. My roommate Abi and I had been putting wet washcloths in the freezer, getting them out just before bedtime and going to sleep on top of our beds with them tucked behind our necks and under our legs. And in the middle of the night, when I'd wake up in the melted-washcloth puddles, I'd walk to the shower, spray my arms and legs down and go back to bed without drying off. It was water that had been simmering in the water tank on the roof all day as the temperatures soared above 100 degrees. But it was better than nothing.

I loved that place. But it was hot, y'all.

It's safe to say we hadn't slept great the morning we woke up early to road trip to Wadi Mujib, an oasis with a cold, clear stream in the rocky Jordanian desert. The stream starts with a roaring, tumbling waterfall and runs through a crevice in steep canyon walls until it hits the warm, salty Dead Sea, and our friend Maurie told us it was one of her favorite places she had ever been.

But it had nothing for me when I woke up that morning. My eyes felt salty when I met Abi in the sweltering hallway between our bedrooms. "I feel like I haven't slept in days," she said. *Me too.*

Neither of us felt like dragging ourselves across the desert. We each wanted to fall back into our respective ovens—bedrooms, rather—and toss and turn in hopes it would eventually feel better. We debated. We changed our minds a couple of times. And we ended up in the car with our friends.

I couldn't be more glad we did. It kind of changed our lives.

When you visit Wadi Mujib, you kind of jump from a staircase above the stream into the rift in the rocks and land in the calm where the water lulls before it moves on to join the sea. Then—all strapped up in a life jacket they provide—you work your way upward to the source. Like a salmon, you wade against the stream with water sometimes waist deep, sometimes ankle deep, sometimes pouring over huge rocks that you have to use a rope to pull yourself up over.

To say we were ready was an understatement.

We might've been reluctant to leave our sunbaked apartment, but once the water was in sight, we were all racing to get there. Where the stream pooled at the base of the crack in the mountain, we hit it at full tilt. We didn't care that, in that context, we probably shouldn't be drawing that much attention to ourselves.

We had been craving this for what felt like a thousand dry, hot months.

It was one of my favorite days of my life.

THERE FOR THE TAKING

That's the way it feels when you finally dive into God's Word and quench the thirst you've always had, the one that, up until now, you've tried to satiate with smaller things. When you go to the Word not for direction but for God Himself, the truth of who He is hits that gnawing in your soul right at the core.

It's peace so deep, cold, and clear that it catches your dry heart off guard.

That's the peace Paul held out to the Athenians the day he told them he had a new God for them to meet, One who would shake their idols, turn their world upside down, and change everything. They would no longer need to sacrifice anything to anyone else and come back still empty. They would no longer have to participate in hedonistic rituals that fell short of the fulfillment they were meant to have.

All this was for the taking—if they would just decide Paul's God was worth meeting.

It's the same for us. When we hear that God is the Creator of everything, the One who holds the stars in His hands, the One who holds our very lives and gives them infinite purpose, we really have only two options: we can mock and turn away as some of the Athenians did, or we can choose to dive in with everything we have. We can't dabble in the God of the universe. As Paul said, there will be a day when we will be held to account for how we chose to live (Acts 17:31). But why would we ever choose to dabble in the world, sacrificing pieces of our hearts to other gods when only one matters, when only one offers pure joy?

WE HAVE TO CHOOSE

The day I hit the water at Wadi Mujib, I threw myself in with abandon, laughed harder than I'd laughed in ages, ran underneath the waterfall like a kid, and then floated on my back all the way back to the base as if I didn't have a care in the world. I had nothing but thirst, and I found nothing but wonder.

And I almost didn't go. Trying to sleep in a baking hot room had sounded better in the moment—and it almost won.

So often real thirst can get crowded out by other things—the things here that distract us or seem more pressing. I have to choose to go to the water's edge. I have to choose to dive into His Word for myself. I have to choose to stop dulling the thirst and give it to Him, just as it is, all of it. I have to let the thirst ache. I have to let Him draw me in.

It's there the thirst comes alive—when I plunge into Him through His Word. Nowhere else. It's where hope begins.

So in the morning, when your baking hot oven of a bedroom seems better, take yourself to the water's edge. Cultivate thirst for the one true God. Then give that thirst back to Him as an offering.

He will never disappoint.

AS YOU PRAY

- Ask God to grow in your heart a thirst for everything He is.
- Ask Him to give you wisdom in how to study the Word and to seek out solid resources and mentors to help you deepen your study of the Word, to understand its intended meaning and context, and let that inform your view of who God is.
- Ask Him to make your thirst one that drinks with joy until it's satisfied and overflows to others.

Day 15
We Find Our Identity in Him

I wasn't there. So I didn't get a nametag. But my friend Elizabeth tells me that if I had been there, in addition to my name, I would have written what I was thankful for on my nametag. But I wouldn't have been allowed to write something normal like family, friends, or home—everybody's thankful for that stuff. And whatever I wrote needed to have a story that could be told around the dinner table.

What did hers say? *Publix.*

It wasn't her best material, but she said it would do, because long story short, the grocery store chain saved Friendsgiving—my friend group's celebration of Thanksgiving. Thanks to one final quick trip to Publix, a lot of friends who decided to come at the last minute got to eat and write nametags with things they were thankful for.

I know at that same moment I was thankful for ten-minute breaks.

Because while my friends were celebrating Thanksgiving, I was working a shift at a coffeehouse, and my ten-minute breaks were a true blessing. I would stand outside and let the cold hit my arms, my breath curling in the air, taking a few moments of rest.

I was sad to miss Friendsgiving. I love my friends, and I hated to not be there.

But I was making coffee that night. And that . . . that I don't hate.

There are all kinds of reasons why. I was in an interesting season of my life. I'd joked that I'd found myself in charge of coffee, people, and money—three things I'd never wanted to be in charge of. My life had formerly been a lot of putting words together, and in this season it was a lot of steaming milk and making espressos. It was a lot of being really, really stretched. It was a lot of people . . . and a lot of stories. And those people and stories etched themselves on my heart, just like the coffee smell that's permanently written on my clothes—and that I love.

It's funny. This season is a part of my story I never would have expected at thirty-five. It's different from anything I ever planned to do.

But one thing I wake up and learn a little more every day is that this wild and crazy story God is writing for us has a lot of incredible depth and a lot of incredible, unexpected twists if we will just hand it all to Him and hang on. Not to the stuff—to Him and to His story.

Because when it comes down to it, we were made for Him. We were made for His story. And God is pretty amazing.

I BELONG TO ANOTHER

When Paul showed up on the scene at the Areopagus, that's what he held out to the people—the offer of a better love and a better story. God had made them, and Paul reminded them that He continued to hold them together, their very life and breath, even in that very moment.

God didn't just create them and leave them—He defined them. He defines us even now. The fact that He made me—and made me for Himself—changes every part of my life. It means who I am doesn't rest in what I have or don't have. It means my very identity lies not in what I do or whatever season I'm in—whether writer or barista, single or widow—it rests in a God in whom I live and move and have my being. I'm a beloved child of God, created in love by Him and rescued in love by His Son, Jesus.

And both of those things mean my life is not my own. I pick up my cross and follow Him, as He asks. And I trust His dream for my life and for the world over my own dreams. Culture might tell me that I need certain things or that I'm owed certain things, a certain kind of life. But what God promises is so much bigger than that, if we will just lay all those expectations down to follow Him into His story with abandon.

We don't need a certain life. We just need Him. If we have Him, it doesn't matter what life looks like—our heart is secure, and we know our seasons have purpose. And we live in the overflow of that. We walk through His story with confidence.

His story is pretty great. It has been for a long time. And there's still a lot left to go. *I want a piece of that.* It starts and ends in the Bible, and my coffeehouse is right there in the middle. Not literally, of course. But all the parts of God's story go together into a living, breathing whole. All the parts, messy as they are, are a seamless story of redemption with Jesus at the center, and a life without night, without tears still to come (Revelation 21–22).

AN ENDING WORTH RUNNING TOWARD

Every night as I locked the café doors, I remembered . . . *God sees me.* He sees me just as much as He saw Ruth in that wheat field even though she was a foreigner, as much as He saw the prostitute who saved His spies' lives, as much as He saw the man born blind.

And the people He saw back then—the stories of who He is and how He saw them—are changing me. As a friend said the other day, reading the Bible really is kind of like reading a story . . . it's just that unlike all the other books we read, the story is true and can change our lives.

It is. It can. It does. It makes your heart pound. It wakes your soul up. It gives you an ending to wait for. And it makes your today come alive.

I love it. And that's what I would've written on my nametag, what I'm thankful for—unexpected twists, and the God who writes them. Every single one is part of the story—a living, breathing story—and every single one of them gets us to Him. He holds our eternal future, and He holds the path that gets us there, no matter what it looks like.

And that's the best part of all.

AS YOU PRAY

- Ask God to remind you of who you are in Him, regardless of what your life looks like or doesn't look like.
- Ask Him to illuminate the Bible as you read it so you can know more and more of who He is and live secure in the fact that you are His.
- Ask Him to give your heart a sense of momentum so that your life is headed toward the future He has for you and everything that happens here is preparing you for that.

Day 16
We Chase Him with Our Whole Lives

TODAY'S READING:
REVELATION 21—22

The wind rushed around the sleeper train, kicking up dust on both sides of the tracks. I had a good view of the unnatural dust storm from where I lay on the third bunk, up in the nosebleed section. My feet dangled off the end of the too-short bed into the aisle, and I checked to see how close I was to kicking people in the face as they walked by.

Not close. Not close at all. I felt miles above their heads. I'd never make foot-to-face contact from way up here. I wasn't going to be Jackie Chan, not even accidentally, not even in my sleep. *It's a long way down*, I thought, and I scooted closer to the wall.

Two bunks below me, the woman across from Elizabeth was offering her some of the noodles she had brought from home in a plastic bag. In the few minutes since we had boarded the train, Elizabeth had become best friends with the noodle lady, plus every baby on the train. Moms would come walking down the aisle looking for Elizabeth, babies in their arms, just so they could grab their little ones' hands and make them wave and watch her wave back.

Up here above head level, above baby-waving level, no one could get to my little pocket of space. And that was kind of nice. Kind of quiet. It gave me space to think. As I lay there listening to the train rush along the tracks, all kinds of thoughts invaded my head and heart, as if the wind was stirring them up on the way by. The depth and breadth of the memories of the past several years exploded in my mind like a kaleidoscope.

God, we've covered a lot of miles since this journey started. All kinds of emotions welled up. My first impulse was to hold everything down where it belonged, slapping my hands down on the memories as if they were napkins on the table of a café on a windy day. But as I lay there staring at the ceiling, I didn't. I didn't hold them down.

I let things fly. This was the space to do that. And it was a good thing. *Because God was in all of those things.*

RACING IS THE ONLY OPTION

Sometimes we need to process what God has done, the places we've walked. Sometimes we need that space on the third bunk up, a place where the daily grind fades away for a little while. Sometimes we need to stop, take a good, long look over our shoulders and remember where God has brought us and who He has been.

There are two reasons for that—at least two main ones. For starters, we're forgetful. We forget where God has brought us and how faithful He's been, just as the people of Israel forgot that God Himself had parted the Red Sea for them to walk through on dry land. And forgetting yesterday makes us look at today and tomorrow and tremble.

But another reason we need to look back over our shoulder is simply to remember *we're in forward motion*. It's so easy to let time sit still, to get so caught up in mundane days and Netflix nights that we forget we're speeding down the tracks toward somewhere.

From God's perspective, chasing Him has always been just that—*chasing*. It has forward motion. It has momentum toward heaven and eternity with Him. It's a race that requires things like endurance, things like throwing off the weights that hold us back (Hebrews 12:1–2). It requires perseverance.

Because when we get to the end, we don't just slide into heaven and check in with a numb mind. God says, "The one who *conquers* will have this heritage, and I will be his God and he will be my son" (Revelation 21:7, emphasis added). Conquering implies active, forward motion.

So we chase God, throwing off the things that hold us back, running headlong into the path He's set before us.

HE CHANGES US

The other day, I came across some things I'd jotted down years ago, back when I'd first said, *God, whatever it takes to know You more, that's what I want.* The girl who wrote that had no idea what was coming—and that's a really good thing. I think I knew it would be incredible. I think I also knew it would be hard. But I don't think I could have ever imagined just how incredible or just how hard. The list of things I couldn't have predicted back then could go on for days. Mountaintops. Miracles. Tragedies. Joy. Grief. Hope. Salvation. He was in all of those things.

And in every moment, every day, He answered my prayer, even though I didn't have a clue what I was really asking for—He gave more of Himself.

Through His Word, He reshaped the way I viewed Him, and that changed the way experiences changed me. My life began to shape itself around who He is in a way that's held its shape even in the moments when He felt farther away, when the really deep waters came. I'm not the same shape I was when I was that wide-eyed girl who wrote down that prayer. I won't be the same shape ten years from now either. That's because of who He is. It's because of His faithfulness, because of His unshakable pursuit of me. And it's because of what happens when He invades the spaces of my life, my heart. I'm changed when I chase Him back.

As I lay there on the train thinking about the experiences that did the molding, the places where His grace held me, the moments of pure joy that sent me to my knees in gratitude, I was overwhelmed. It's a big, big bag—of deep, deep gratitude.

What will the next ten years bring? I can't imagine. But I want it. *If it gives me more of You, I want it. I don't want to stay the same. I want Your story, whatever that means. I want the story that leads me to You.*

It's time for us to get up, strengthen our weak knees, make straight paths for our feet . . . and chase (Hebrews 12:12).

AS YOU PRAY

- Ask God to capture your heart with the race He's got for you to run—the one that leads you to Him.
- Ask Him to help you remember His faithfulness in the past—both to you and those who have gone before you—and to remember He will still be faithful today and in the future.
- Ask Him to fill your heart up with the truth of His Word to remind you that you're in a race, a race with an incredible destination.

Day 17
He Speaks to Us

TODAY'S READING:
ACTS 17:27–28

The laundry hangs dead still on the line just outside the window screen. It's a good thing a breeze isn't the mark of success here. The air sits heavy, dry, and hot as it would in a convection oven, and though there's no wind, moisture evaporates so fast you can almost hear it leaving.

Perspiration beads on my face as I sit beside Mu, tearing cabbage much more slowly than she does. "Clare was probably much better at this than me," I say. Her dark eyes laugh, but the laughter doesn't make it to her mouth. "You're doing great," she says instead, grinning.

We smile, but we have a common hurt—our friend Clare had traveled from England to spend months working at a school in Southeast Asia before she passed away. While she was there, she'd spent hours in that kitchen with Mu. She misses Clare too.

We carry on in silence, ripping leaf after leaf, until a bird squawks through the screen, a bird that sounds even closer than the laundry. I jump. "Your birds are really interesting here," I say. What I mean is . . . *your birds are a little bit crazy here.*

That morning, I had lain in bed with my eyes open, listening to the cacophony of jungle sounds outside the window, including one bird that sounded like a screaming toddler. Every time its voice raked against my window, I shot up from the sheets.

"Did you hear them this morning when you were in bed?" Mu asks. I smile. "I did."

"At 4 a.m.?"

Oh no, not that early. I tell her as much. "Oh, good," she says. Apparently the neighbor has a rooster that likes to wake everyone up. And apparently that same neighbor also likes to feed rice to the entire country's population of crows in her driveway every morning.

No wonder I felt as if I'd woken up in a bird sanctuary.

Even if the neighbor wasn't the birds' main breakfast supplier, I still couldn't blame them for flocking here every day. The former owner of the house where we sat ripping cabbage used to keep the upstairs window open, letting the birds have the whole second floor to themselves to do as they pleased. When she moved out, they got kicked out.

They still peck on the windows. Every day. They haven't forgotten their posh former home.

A HUNGER TO HEAR HIS VOICE

Sitting there in the thick, hot silence of the kitchen, Mu and I can hear the birds loud and clear from where they sit in the trees, some near, some far, all singing a language to each other that neither of us can understand. "Sometimes it really sounds like they're communicating with each other," Mu says. She looks out the screen over the sink, absently washing the cabbage in a small plastic bowl. "You know, one of the things about Clare that I loved the most was the way she communicated with God. It changed the way I communicate with God too. I saw she could really hear Him."

It was as though Clare and God spoke their own language, she said. They heard and understood each other.

When Clare first met Jesus, she was right here in Southeast Asia. And she was overwhelmed by Him and His love. She found it—it found her—in the silence, the simplicity here. She begged Him to speak to her. She was hungrier for Him than anything else. He spoke. And she listened. And she poured out her heart to Him like a close friend, a friend she could talk to naturally, a friend who meant more to her than anything and anyone else.

That stuck with Mu. She started to pray the way Clare did. And in the thick, hot silence that sits around Mu's heart and the house where she prepares dinner, God speaks to her. And she curls up right in the center of it and sits down. Because, just like with Burmese laundry, just like with Elijah in 1 Kings 19, wind isn't always the measure of success. God's voice often isn't in the wind or the earthquake or the fire. Plenty is getting said in the silence.

MEETING GOD'S WHISPER

We know that He's that close, close enough to speak to our hearts when we press into the silence. We know from Paul's letters and so many other places that He's not far from each one of us, near enough that we can reach out for Him and find Him, as Clare did and as Mu did.

That's what Paul himself prayed for us—that we would know God and have confidence in His Spirit living within us. He wrote in Ephesians 3:14–19:

> For this reason I bow my knees before the Father . . . [that] he may grant you to be strengthened with power through his Spirit in your inner being, so that Christ may dwell in your hearts through faith—that you, being rooted and grounded in love, may have strength to comprehend with all the saints what is the breadth and length and height and depth, and to know the love of Christ that surpasses knowledge, that you may be filled with all the fullness of God.

Paul wanted us to be filled with the fullness of God and to know His love for us. That's the message he held out to anyone at the Areopagus who might be willing to listen and look for God. He wanted the Athenians to reach past the cultural noise crowding out the real God and find the truth that was waiting in the quiet.

So that's where we go—the silent spots in our lives. We find them. We wrap our faces as Elijah did, expecting God's presence and glory, and we go there and listen. We make silent places in the midst of chaos, if we have to. We make silent places in our hearts.

And there He finds us. And remakes us. And we find we can communicate.

AS YOU PRAY

- Talk to God as if He's as close as your very breath. He is. And He cares for you.
- Ask God to guide your heart to a constant conversation with Him so that you can pray without ceasing, as Paul said (1 Thessalonians 5:17).
- Ask Him to give you opportunities to talk to others about the real relationship you have with God so they can perhaps desire to have one too.

Day 18
We Trust His Path

TODAY'S READING:
DEUTERONOMY 31:6; PSALM 56:8

It was a normal week, the week they found a spot on my dad's lung. A tiny spot, about the size of the piece of grit that fell out of my shoe when I'd gone for a walk earlier that same week. When I finally stopped and shook the annoyance out, it hit the pavement like lint, soundless and light. In the moments before it fell out into the sunshine, it had ground into my heel like an ice pick. I'm always amazed at how something so tiny can feel so big sometimes.

Dad's spot had popped up on a routine scan, a little piece of grit, unknown and dark. We didn't know how long it had been there. We didn't know what it was. And that was scary. As I lay in bed that night, things rolling around in my mind, I rolled over on my side, pulled the covers over my head, and curled my knees up to my chest. And from my tiny dark spot, I whispered. "God, You see it right? That spot—You see it? And You see me too?"

I had felt as though there had been a few things that had popped up lately, little dark spots I didn't quite know how to handle. Spots that made me uncomfortable and I felt unequipped to deal with. Spots I didn't love. And I'd curled up under the covers more than a few times, right into those spots, and I'd wondered—*is that spot outside God's line of sight?*

I knew it wasn't true—nothing escapes His view. But subconsciously I'd been treating some of them like that, and consequently they had been rubbing me raw, boring into my soul like ice picks in my running shoes. It's as though I thought that spot was the one place where maybe He wasn't going to be who He says He is. Or maybe it was the one place in my life where He just wouldn't come through, that He just wouldn't be enough. Or maybe the spot where God brought me to save me is now the spot where He's going to leave me to figure it out on my own.

HE NEVER, EVER LEAVES US ALONE

All of us who know Jesus have been in that spot—the one where He rescued and redeemed us. That's the spot Paul was talking about when he told the Athenians that God had been determining the periods and boundaries of people's lives so they could get there—that they might seek Him and feel their way toward Him and find Him.

But for those of us who threw our hands up in that place and gave Him everything, we have to know: He didn't take it all and run. He didn't leave us there alone. He said *keep running. I'm right here.*

That was Moses's charge to Joshua when God's people were first beginning to walk into the land God had promised them. Moses was passing the baton to Joshua as leader, and his biggest piece of advice was, "Be strong and courageous. . . . For it is the Lord your God who goes with you. He will not leave you or forsake you" (Deuteronomy 31:6). It didn't matter what

Joshua was going to face on this journey that God was taking him on—he would never be alone. There would never be a moment when God didn't see him, and—even better—there would never be a moment when God didn't care.

In Him we live and move and have our being—He is not far from any one of us. That includes that spot under the covers. That includes my worry over the spot in my dad's lung. It includes all the other spots that ever have been and ever will be. He's never left us alone. And He never will.

He sees. He knows. He loves.

LETTING THINGS HERE FADE

It's a beautiful thing for Christ followers, the way we're rescued one day from the gnawing in our soul and suddenly realize we have everything we could ever need all wrapped up in the One who made us. We've got infinite love, joy, mercy. We've got the Holy Spirit guiding us, planting heaven in our hearts, urging us on. We've got Him illuminating Scripture so we can meet Him as we read and see Him for who He really is.

We don't go it alone.

There's not a bend in our road He doesn't see coming. There's no enemy we'll face that He isn't ready for. There's no pain that surprises Him. There's no grief too big for Him to carry you through.

Remember that promise as you face obstacles that seem big in your life, the trials that bore into your soul like ice picks. Remember that promise when days hurt. Remember that promise when situations seem hazy or scary or unknown. Remember when you're lonely: He's never left you alone. He keeps your tears in a bottle, a tender mercy that reminds us He sees. He knows exactly how many times you toss and turn in the night. He holds your very breath in His hands. And that isn't a distant concept—it's a sign of His very present affection for you. Every little ice pick you feel, it's not meant to push you away; it's meant to pull you further in, to pull you to Him so He can fill you up with more of Himself.

Following Him down the steps of this broken world brings pain—we're told that over and over. But it also brings unspeakable joy, here just a foretaste, there one day with Him in its fullness. And as we trust Him with our path, it also brings the opportunity to cultivate a relationship here that makes the miles we walk feel more and more temporary compared to what's to come. We look forward to seeing Him face to face. We yearn for it with everything in us. It's a different kind of gnawing (2 Corinthians 5:1–5).

It's the kind that, when we curl up under the covers in the dark, we say, "Even here, God—even this part of the path is Yours. And You're with me."

AS YOU PRAY

- Ask God to strengthen you with His Word every morning so when the tough spots come, they drive you further into the truth you know about Him.
- Thank Him for the way He set His affection on you.
- Ask Him to give you confidence in the truth of His presence as you walk through your day today.

Day 19
We Can't Turn Back

The sun poured down through the thousands of dead brown leaves rustling together in the trees, our own surround-sound percussion section. The breeze turned the pages of my journal, and my friend, Caitlin, dozed with her head on her arm on the other side of the picnic table.

It felt like summer in the middle of winter. Kids were playing baseball. Families were walking their dogs. It was January in Alabama.

And it was great.

There isn't a lot that makes sense with the weather here in winter. For a few days in a row that week in late January, the sun kept baking Birmingham, and the temperature topped 70 degrees. People were fanning themselves in the coffee shop where I worked. The cup was half full of winter, half full of summer. And the summer half was winning. I wasn't sad about that.

The breeze rattled the trees again, and then it happened. I heard it. It was faint, but it was unmistakable.

The ice cream truck.

Before the first note had even died out, Caitlin's head shot up from her arm, her face lit up like Christmas morning. Only a few days before, I'd told her one of those things you hate to admit out loud. I had never actually had ice cream from an ice cream truck. I know, I know. It's un-American and all. But the small town where I grew up didn't have one, so I didn't get the whole experience of sprinting out the front door at the first note, afraid you might not catch it.

I didn't really feel as though I'd missed out on any-thing. And Caitlin thought that was just wrong. So that day, we chased the ice cream man. The first time we ran across the bridge and through the park, leaving all our belongings behind.

We didn't make it. We trudged back to our picnic table. But about fifteen minutes later, we heard the music again, and we did it all over again. And this time we caught him.

I'd tuned that jingle out for more than thirty years. But because of that summer day in January, I never would be able to again.

ONCE YOU'VE TASTED IT

A few days before, Caitlin and I were talking about how some-times the depths of following after Christ can be deep, if you really want to know Him for all He's worth. If you want to grab hold of Him, it's not something you just accidentally slide into while you're living your life. You have to really want it.

The battle can be rough. The difficult things can be really difficult. And sometimes life might just seem simpler if you stayed at the picnic table and didn't have to make that full-out sprint.

But you would also never know the soul-shaking joy and all-consuming peace that comes from running after Him with lungs burning, heart pumping—and catching Him. Once you taste it, it's as if the picnic table life is never an option you'll be OK with again.

Caitlin said it's like once you know what Jesus is really like, trying to go back to living that life without Him isn't going to work. "It might've worked then when I didn't know the alternative, but now that I do, it throws everything off when I try to revert back," she said. "Much like when I was introduced to the ice cream man—before I knew who he was, my life was fine and happy, but after I knew who he was, I couldn't just go back to not knowing and be happy as I was before. I craved ice cream."

I knew what she meant. It's not always easy, this road. In fact, a lot of the time it's hard. But the deep depths pale in light of the high highs.

And she's right. You can't go back.

WHERE ELSE WOULD WE GO?

There were several moments in Jesus' time on earth that, while He was walking, He turned around and realized a crowd was following Him. This happened in John 6 just after He had broken five loaves of bread and two fish and miraculously multiplied the pieces to feed a crowd of thousands. He turned to the people and knew their hearts—He knew most of them didn't really see Him for who He was, just for what He could give them. So He said to them, "Truly, truly, I say to you, you are seeking me, not because you saw signs, but because you ate your fill of the loaves" (v. 26). He told them not to waste their lives on bread that passes away but instead to waste themselves completely for the bread of eternal life, the bread that lasts forever—Jesus Himself.

> **I am the bread of life; whoever comes to me shall not hunger, and whoever believes in me shall never thirst. But I said to you that you have seen me and yet do not believe. All that the Father gives me will come to me, and whoever comes to me I will never cast out.**
>
> **—vv. 35–37**

They had asked, "What must we do, to be doing the works of God?" (v. 28). But Jesus knew they weren't ready to give their lives. And so He told them a hard truth about losing themselves by taking on His soon-to-be crucified life, "Whoever feeds on my flesh and drinks my blood has eternal life, and I will raise him up on the last day" (v. 54).

When many people in the crowd heard that, they walked away.

So Jesus asked His twelve disciples, "Do you want to go away as well?" (v. 67). But Peter said, "Lord, to whom shall we go? You have the words of eternal life, and we have believed, and have come to know, that you are the Holy One of God" (vv. 68–69). Peter might have had a lot to figure out, but one thing was sure—he had seen Jesus, and he knew the only life worth having when he saw it. The more he chased Christ and Christ alone, the more his life became about knowing Him and sharing Him with others. He became Paul's counterpart in the Book of Acts, sharing the gospel boldly with the Jews while Paul was living a parallel storyline with the Gentiles, or non-Jews.

Peter knew life when he saw it. We follow in his steps, and Paul's too. Where would we go? After we've tasted eternal life, what pull do the small things have anymore? They try constantly to weigh down our souls, but the song of Christ in our hearts rings out, pulling us to drop it all and keep sprinting.

Lord, to whom would we go? The world has nothing for us. In Christ, we have the only prize worth having, and He tells us that if we're His, He will never cast us out.

And so we press on.

AS YOU PRAY

- Ask God to plant His song in your heart so that, if your affections are distracted, they are drawn quickly back.
- Ask Him to give you the vigilance and determination to shed the things that weigh you down.
- Ask Him to give you continued strength, endurance, and fullness of heart for the race He has drawn you to run.

Day 20
He Gives Light, and We Pass It On

It was dark in the tiny apartment living room, except for the florescent desk lamp, cocked upward, straining to fill the room with as much light as it could.

People were packed in every dim corner.

Leaving their shoes in a neat heap at the door, people squeezed in, sitting reverently on mismatched furniture provided by strangers before the apartment's residents ever set foot on American soil. A few spoke English well. A few spoke it somewhat, others not at all.

All spoke Nepali.

Just a few months ago, they were refugees, living on the border between Nepal and Bhutan until the United Nations decided to bring them to the Atlanta, Georgia, area. "We say we don't have citizenship anywhere—we are citizens of heaven," twenty-seven-year-old Batsa said. They were Nepalese, then Bhutanese, then American. They were refugees first, then believers, then disciples.

And now disciplers.

PASSING IT ON

Ben—a Georgia boy—faced the small group of believers, his head silhouetted by the desk lamp, and began to share with them the story of Nicodemus, the idea of rebirth, and the glorious message of John 3:16. They knew going in that they would hear this sermon three times. Ben told it to them, and Batsa translated. Then Batsa taught it himself to the group in impassioned Nepali. Then they all helped retell it a third time.

The repetition wasn't just for good measure. Chimini, Batsa's sister, would be teaching it the next night in the home of a Hindu priest where two women had recently accepted Christ. Batsa also led a house church for Nepalis. Two others in the room taught groups of their own.

And in the small, fledgling group of believers, there was still need for one more tonight.

"We've had the opportunity to have another Bible study in someone's home, and I want you to be praying about whether or not God is speaking to your heart about you being the one to lead it," Ben said.

To these Nepali believers, that's what it meant to be the Church—they learned for themselves, but they also learned so they could pass it on to others.

"What did you learn from the story of Nicodemus?" Ben asked them.

Batsa said he thought the story would speak to people with Hindu beliefs, who might have burning questions inside as he used to before he met Christ. Questions like, if people have to buy things to get right with their hundreds of millions of gods, how could poor people ever afford to get to god? Could Jesus, who loves the whole world, be that easy to get to?

A young Nepali boy raised his hand and, pointing to the desk lamp, said, "I learned people live in darkness until they get in the light."

Ben broke into a huge grin. I couldn't blame him. It's a dim apartment—but the Light from it shines pretty amazingly bright.

TURNING THE WORLD UPSIDE DOWN

Today, more than 200 million people live outside their country of birth. If that mass of people collectively were a single country, they would represent the fifth-largest nation in the world. They're people like Batsa and Chimini. And again and again, they are providentially bumping into the truth, finding the light, and then sharing it with others.

That's what citizens of heaven do.

Not too long before Paul arrived in Athens, he and his traveling companion Silas stopped in Thessalonica to share the Light with the Jews there. They wanted desperately for them to believe Jesus was the Christ, so week after week they went to the synagogue and showed them evidence from the Scriptures. Some believed, but others were jealous of their influence, so they went to the authorities to try to shut the movement down. Their accusation? Paul and Silas were turning the world upside down. Like Batsa and Chimini, all they had done was see the Light and tell others what they'd learned.

Paul didn't complicate matters, but he did do this—he chased people. He chased them in his own hometown, and he took long trips to find them. He looked for them right where they were. For Jews, that meant the synagogue on the day they worshipped. For Greeks, that meant Mars Hill, the place they gathered to share ideas.

For Paul, chasing the God who had chased him first meant that he began to love what God loved.

And that meant people.

OUR MINUTES ARE HIS

So what does it look like to chase after people in our neighborhoods, our jobs, our schools? How do we live with intentionality, taking the minutes of our everyday life captive for the sake of the people around us still held captive by the darkness?

We fall in love with the God who chases us in the pages of His Word, and we give Him everything.

For some of us in certain seasons—or maybe for an entire lifetime—we'll follow Him to a different city or country so people who may have been living and dying in darkness for generations might see Light for the first time. God's Word demands that we consider it—we've been entrusted with Light, and they haven't. How could we not?

For some of us, it may mean we get a job that puts us around people who don't know Jesus so that they can see something different and be drawn to the gospel. For some, it may mean you take the kids to play every day at the neighborhood park just so you can start to build relationships with other moms.

In every situation, it means we get up in the mornings and say, "God, my minutes are Yours—give me eyes to see the people You want me to see today." We pray for Him to bring people across our paths. We pray for Him to deepen our love for the lost and our desire to go find them.

And we read and press in to God so we can pass the truth of who He is to others.

AS YOU PRAY

- Thank God for the people He used to bring light into your life.
- Ask God to help you start to see your whole life with intentionality, both the necessary and mundane and the bold, new adventures. Ask Him to use you right where you are and anywhere else He chooses.
- Ask Him to bring people into your path today who are in need of the peace and light God offers. Ask Him to help you take steps today in the direction of building purposeful relationships.

Day 21
He Calls Us to
Build Bridges

"She can speak a little English. Just speak really slowly." And with that, my friend Katie left the room. And there I was, staring at her friend, her dark eyes nervous in her olive face. I smiled.

She smiled back. It went OK for the swap of a few simple phrases. Then we hit a lull.

And I thought . . . *here we go. Here's where it starts to get interesting.*

If you had asked me a few months prior what nation of people in the world I thought I might have the least in common with, I probably would have picked this one. Now, even after a couple of days there, I could see that wasn't true. We weren't polar opposites . . . but I still wouldn't say we had much common ground. I tried to think of anything I could ask her in simple English, and in the moment, I was drawing a blank.

"I heard it is your mother's birthday tomorrow," I said finally, enunciating each word.

She stared at me in confusion.

I said it more slowly and added "and there's going to be a party" at the end, as if that would somehow make it more clear. I thought she didn't understand me, but as I was trying to regroup a second time, slowly she said, "I don't know when my mother's birthday is."

"Oh." I smiled and laughed a bit. Obviously I had gotten her mixed up with someone else on the whole party thing. Turns out it was the mother of a different friend I'd been told about.

Now I was the one who didn't understand.

If an American friend had told me she didn't know when her mom's birthday was, it would probably just mean she didn't have her smartphone calendar close at hand. But what my new friend meant was that her *mom* didn't know when her birthday was. And this friend didn't know when her own birthday was either.

THE LAND WITHOUT BIRTHDAYS

It's not that it's an uncivilized place—it's a country where women get university degrees in computer science, wear high heels and shirts with trendy English slogans, go bowling for fun, and notice if their friends' eyebrows aren't threaded well enough.

But I understood better when I met her mom a few days later. I was a guest in her family's home—one of the best meals I'd had in a long time, spread on the kitchen floor for probably fifteen of us, rice and vegetables and this fabulous dish that was like lamb meat in the middle of fried cornbread.

The matriarch of the family was timid and beautiful, sitting on the floor in a loose dress with her head covered, not speaking much. After a little while, through the translation of a friend, she quietly began to tell the story about how, when their city was attacked by outsiders years ago, she had to split up the family and they fled for their lives over the mountains. On donkeys.

Some of her children went one direction with relatives, and some went with her the other direction. One was born en route—she hiked while in labor, had the baby, then kept hiking. Some of the children she didn't see again until several years later, and they didn't recognize her anymore when they were reunited.

It's been a story of fear, violence, and fleeing for generations. Few people know their real birthdays.

It seems hard to relate when you put it that way.

But at the same time, it's easy. They're beautiful people who love their families, their country, their food, and their friends just as much as I do.

It was just going to take some time and effort to lovingly build some bridges.

STUDENTS OF THE CULTURE

Paul said to the Jews he became a Jew and to the weak he became weak so that people could come to know the gospel with as few cultural roadblocks as possible (1 Corinthians 9:20–22). And Jesus Himself modeled service and humility when it came to relationships, ministry, and life.

That's why missionaries study their new countries before they ever go overseas, then become active students of the culture the moment they arrive. They watch. They listen. They ask questions. They want to know how to build bridges between themselves and their people group—to break down the barriers so they can share Jesus more easily.

That's what Paul did in Athens—he had been a student of their philosophy and poetry to the point he could quote it and use it as a bridge to the message of Jesus. He found the things they had in common and started there. And he studied the culture enough to know what the Athenians' questions would be, and he answered them.

And that's what we should do, even if the United States is home. We know we're in the world and not of it, but we should at least be in it—engaged in the culture so we can reach the people who live around us.

Because when it comes down to it, everyone has that hunger, that gnawing in his or her soul to know God. That's common to all people—much like the remnants of the image of God that show up in a variety of ways, like proclaimed atheists having a desire to make the world better or a nonreligious person having compassion for others.

But oftentimes to reach into that space where the struggle is happening, where the gnawing is real, we have to invest our time. We have to see their souls as valuable, investing our time in studying like Paul did so that we can have good, rich, informed conversations. We study other things that are important to us—why not study other people so that, perhaps, by all means possible we can save some as Paul did?

It takes effort. When we decide losing weight is important, we force ourselves off the couch and outside for a walk. When we decide knowing God is important, we set the alarm and discipline ourselves to get up and pray and read His Word.

And when we decide people are important, we take the time to study them and learn what's important to them so we can sincerely and thoughtfully engage them.

So we offer ourselves alongside the gospel, like Paul in Thessalonica. We show people we're like them but so different at the exact same time. We pray they see the difference and want it for themselves. And we ask God to guide our words, our lives, our everything.

AS YOU PRAY

- Ask God to help you have an awareness of the people and the culture around you.
- Ask Him to give you the drive to study culture, language, and Scripture so you can be ready for conversations with the people you've identified.
- Ask God to help you start new relationships with the purpose of building bridges to the gospel.

Day 22
He Calls Us to Be Bold

TODAY'S READING:
ACTS 17:22–31

Jen couldn't stop crying, and she had no idea why. It made zero sense. And that drove her crazy.

She had decided to try the Bible study because she had gone on a few dates with a guy who was a Christian. She was an atheist—always had been—but she knew it was important to him, so she told him she would go.

Everyone was excited when she showed up. But I wouldn't say we eased her in.

The night she came was the first night of a series on missions, and right out of the gate the topic was how people who live and die without a chance to hear the gospel spend an eternity in hell. The night was burdened with that reality. Everyone sat around talking about the responsibility we all have to go to those places and give them a chance to follow Christ and escape that fate. We talked about how Christians don't take it seriously enough.

We all walked away heavy—but Jen couldn't sleep.

Several weeks later, she told the Bible study leader that she didn't understand why she felt such deep compassion for people who hadn't gotten the opportunity to hear the gospel—a message she herself didn't believe in. That irritated her. If it wasn't real, why did it bother her so much?

It makes us all smile now, but no one would have ever guessed that an intense call to missions would have been the thing that convinced Jen to believe as fast as she did. We all thought she probably wouldn't come back after that week, but the opposite happened.

It struck a chord.

I remember that night after Jen walked out of that first study. We all looked at each other a little nervously and said, "We probably scared her off." We had a moment when we thought it might have been better if it had been a different night, a different topic—a message not any less true but maybe not quite so intense. Up until then, Jen hadn't had the best impression of Christians, and we would've loved a chance to win her over more slowly.

But as it turns out, what happened that night was exactly what needed to happen for Jen to recognize that gnawing in her soul.

She didn't need to be eased in. She needed to hear a truth she had never heard before.

COURAGEOUS TRUTH

That's the way it was that day in Athens, the day Paul addressed the Areopagus. He could have built a bridge by addressing them respectfully and talking about their religion, but he didn't stay there. He also didn't take them by the hand and walk them slowly to Jesus.

He simply shared the radical truth—that the crucified and resurrected Christ was their only way to escape judgment.

It might have seemed a little crazy, but that was the very thing that got him invited to speak to the Areopagus in the first place. He never would have gotten asked to speak there if he wasn't saying something new, something the philosophers had never heard before. He might have connected with them on a spiritual level before he got to the heart of it, but he didn't try to ease them in to the gospel. He wasn't worried about what they thought of him or if they thought he was crazy— something that might not have been the case back when he was living the life of a Jewish scholar.

For him, it was all about Jesus. He was so immersed in the Word of God that he knew his identity and acceptance by God was secure and that in Jesus alone he lived and moved and had his being. He was certain of the Resurrection. He was certain of grace.

And that gave him the courage and freedom to let their opinions go.

RATTLING SOULS, SHAKING IDOLS

That's what Jen needed from us that night. She needed us to connect with her, but she didn't need us to hold her hand and walk her so slowly to Christ that she didn't even remember walking there herself. She didn't need something to add to what she already had, like a nice religious morality that fit just fine with atheism, like an "unknown god" that could be tacked on to Zeus and Athena and everyone else.

She needed to hear something radically different from everything she had ever believed, something that rattled her soul and made her question her unbelief.

She needed the gospel to shake her idols.

We were compassionate and welcoming, I hope—we wanted to be. We tried to be sensitive to her as we studied the topic and divided into groups to talk about it. But we didn't back down from the truth. She knew sitting in our midst that the line was drawn, and she was standing on the other side of it. We all felt it, but what we wanted her to know was that more than anything, we loved her, and we didn't want her to be where she was. We wanted her to know the risen Jesus. And we wanted her to keep meeting with us and wrestling with it until she did.

That's the model Jesus Himself lived by when He walked the earth—He spent time with the people who were farthest from the door of the synagogue, the ones on the other end of the religious spectrum. He knew their culture, ate with them, became friends with them, and even called them to be His disciples—and He didn't back down from the truth. He extended mercy and forgiveness to a woman caught in adultery (John 8:10–11), but He reminded His followers that sin is so serious that if our hand causes us to sin, it would be better for us to cut it off and save ourselves from hell (Mark 9:43). His identity was secure. He could love with abandon, weep over the lostness of Jerusalem, and still not mince words about eternity.

That's the model Paul was walking in when he walked up the Hill of Ares.

And that's the model we should still walk in today.

Are you bold when it comes to sharing the polarizing parts of the gospel, the ones that either draw people to follow or draw them to mock? Have you asked God to help you grow in courage? Have you prepared for these moments? Don't be apathetic about preparing—put your heart into it. Put your time into it. Know the Word to know God, but know it also for the sake of others.

After all, someone—maybe several someones—did that for you.

AS YOU PRAY

- Ask God to give you a hunger for the Word and a motivation to know it well so that you can share it well with others.
- Ask Him to convict you to spend less time on things that don't matter and more time preparing for those moments when you can share truth boldly.
- Ask Him to draw Jens into your life who need to hear the gospel.

Day 23
He Guides Us to People in Need

The fire was crackling in the fireplace and people were milling around with drinks when Angela walked in and slid into a chair at a table in the corner.

It was psychic night at the local pub, an event no more offensive to the general community than a team trivia night or a rugby match on the big screen. People were taking turns conversing with the local psychic, and there in the corner, without drawing any attention to herself at all, Angela sat at her table, sipped her drink, and prayed silently.

For a little while, things carried on like that. But after a few minutes, the psychic got up and walked straight up to Angela's table.

"I know what you're doing," she said. "And I need you to stop, because ever since you've arrived, I haven't been able to see anything."

HUNGRY FOR ANSWERS

Before I'd moved to England, I'd been warned of its postmodern atmosphere—that people there were increasingly cold to the idea of absolute truth or the idea of a God. I'd expected people in my new hometown to be apathetic to all things spiritual.

I was wrong. I don't know if it was just because that psychic from the pub happened to be popular in this one small town or if this kind of thing pervaded the country, but it seemed as though everywhere I turned, people were trying it. Fellow believers were constantly trying to figure out how to talk to their friends about the issue, because their friends keep going to psychics to talk to their dead parents.

The people in our town were hungry for answers. They were desperate to be reconnected with someone they had lost or find some kind of advice or meaning for the future.

They wanted to know there was something greater than themselves.

My driving instructor Nicola—the one who told me about her brother's accident—was one of them. She had prayed for God to spare his life, and when He didn't, she thought maybe there wasn't a God. Her words surprised me—up to that point, she hadn't said much that would lead me to believe she thought much about God at all.

But what she said next surprised me even more. "But after I went to that psychic, I thought there might be a God again." Nicola said the psychic had known everything about her and had even channeled her grandmother. "Freaky stuff," Nicola said. "But it felt very real."

She said she'd been reluctant to tell me because she knew I was "religious," and she didn't think I would believe in it.

I told her I very much believed it was real—I just believed it was very, very dangerous, that it opened the door of her heart to the wrong side, to the demonic. That scared her a little. She hadn't really thought of it that way. She hadn't really seen it as a big deal at all, other than the fact that she was a little freaked out and a lot intrigued.

But it revealed something about her heart—even though she felt as though God had done her wrong when it came to her brother, she wasn't willing to totally shut the door on the idea of a very real spiritual realm.

She wanted answers. She searched for something. And the fact that she hadn't found it yet wasn't enough to satiate the desire to keep looking.

VESSELS FOR TRUTH

When Paul went to Athens, he saw a scene much like Angela found in the pub—people fervently trying anything and everything. Acts 17:16 says that "his spirit was pro-voked within him as he saw that the city was full of idols." The Athenians deeply desired to worship something—they had altar after altar where they could give their lives to something false, something that would keep them in blindness, something that would never save them. They wanted the false promises of their gods to be true. They formed whole groups just to talk about new philosophies they could chase.

They wanted light, but they looked for it from sources that only wanted to steal their souls. They put their lives into ritu-als that invited the presence of darkness into their lives simply because they sought some sort of palpable deliverance.

But graciously, in the midst of their hunger for truth, God sent light.

And He sent it in the vessel of Paul.

Ever since Paul had been ripped from his own spiritual blindness on the road to Damascus, he had been a vessel through which God spoke truth to the hurting, searching, desperate, and blind. The more he grew in his new faith, the more boldly he spoke and the more he "confounded the Jews who lived in Damascus by proving that Jesus was the Christ" (Acts 9:22). When God later sent him on a journey, he courageously arrived in Salamis (a port of Cyprus) with the truth, and immediately a magician named Elymas tried to shut him down. But Paul, "filled with the Holy Spirit, looked intently at him and said, 'You son of the devil, you enemy of all righteousness, full of all deceit and villainy, will you not stop making crooked the straight paths of the Lord? And now, behold, the hand of the Lord is upon you, and you will be blind and unable to see the sun for a time'" (Acts 13:9–11).

What Paul said happened. And the people who saw it believed in God.

REDEEMED WITH A PURPOSE

The spiritual landscape we walk into on a daily basis is marked with the opposition of the enemy—this we know. But we also know it is marked with hearts that hurt, hearts that long to be free of the chains that bind them. And if there's one thing we can be certain of, it's that God expects us to go to them.

God didn't redeem Paul for the sake of Paul alone—He redeemed him so He could send him out to push back the darkness and rescue the dying.

He redeems us for the same reason. He wants us to go out like Angela in the power of prayer and intercede for them, to risk pain and prison and even death like Paul and preach the truth in hopes that it meets them at the place where they are searching for God.

He wants us to love them, to have a burden for them to find what we've found. That's all part of being His. *How else will they know?*

God loves us personally, yes. He redeems us in love.

But He also redeems us so He can love others through us.

So like Paul, we enter their corner of the world with intentionality, armed with the truth of the gospel and the power of the Holy Spirit. We don't go alone—we go with the knowledge that God sends us, He will never leave us, and He's the One who opens hearts and does the work to change them. We're merely the vessel.

But what a privilege.

AS YOU PRAY

- Ask God to give you an awareness of the spiritual need of people around you and an urgency to share Jesus with them.
- Ask Him to put people in your path who are searching for God, whose hearts are soft to hear. Ask Him to give you eyes to see opportunities and boldness to share with the people you encounter.
- Ask God to push back Satan's hold on hearts all over the world so they can accept the truth of the gospel.

Day 24
He Brings Purpose in Persecution

TODAY'S READING:
ACTS 16:16–40

It had seemed like a normal day at first. Meleeka and her father were riding in the car on their way to one of her English classes, and she noticed they were being followed. She drummed her fingers nervously on the car door. Her dad kept on driving the familiar route, singing a praise song as he drove.

Meleeka turned around and looked back. "Dad. We're being followed."

He sang louder. Meleeka started to panic. "Would you take it seriously?"

Not missing a beat, he changed his lyrics mid-verse and belted out a song of his own—"I'm going to prison today!"

He knew the signs. He had already been in prison once for his faith in Jesus. In the region where Meleeka and her family lived, people bend over backward to show hospitality. Go to your neighbors' home, and they will spread out a feast for you and heap your plate high with special food. Leave your wallet somewhere, and people will guard it until you return. In their country, people take care of each other.

But share Christ openly, and they may torture you.

Meleeka herself was targeted after her dad's arrest, but she fled to the United States. Her dad lost dozens of pounds in prison, and after months of torture, he was finally released.

But he gained a lot of new brothers. People listened to him inside the walls of that prison. The gospel went forth from there in the most unexpected ways—in the hearts and the mouths of former terrorists. Nearly forty men came to faith as a result of his time in jail. There's no way to know the intricate plans of God, but it's possible Meleeka's father's imprisonment is the only way those men would have ever crossed paths with someone who could point them to Jesus.

It was worth it, Meleeka's father says. Worth every minute in prison. Worth every bit of persecution. Worth missing those years with his family. It was worth it for the glory and the gospel of Jesus Christ.

And it was worth it for the men he will see again in heaven.

A HIGH-COST ROAD, WITH GREAT REWARD

Meleeka's father wasn't the first to see God pursue the lost in the midst of the persecution of His followers. Paul himself had tasted prison just a few cities before he arrived in Athens and had seen God redeem others through that experience. He had been trying to get to Bithynia, but the Spirit of Jesus had stopped him (Acts 16:7)—He bent Paul's path instead in the direction of Philippi, a leading city in the district of Macedonia.

Paul knew his purpose, and he made use of the time there. He spoke with the women gathered together at the riverside, and God opened the heart of a woman named Lydia so the truth of Jesus Christ could rush into her heart and change her (vv. 14–15). He made Lydia's path collide with Paul's, and as a result she found hope.

It's the kind of story we all want.

But as Paul and his companions walked on from there, things got tougher. A slave girl who told fortunes followed them, shouting, "These men are servants of the Most High God, who proclaim to you the way of salvation" (v. 17). Day after day she did this until finally Paul got so annoyed he couldn't handle it anymore. She had a spirit living in her—that was why she was able to tell fortunes—and Paul knew the spirit wasn't on their side. He skipped confronting the slave girl and went straight to the source. He told the spirit, "I command you in the name of Jesus Christ to come out of her" (v. 18).

And it did.

Seems like a good end to the story. The girl's soul was free, and Paul was free to preach in peace. But then the girl's owners realized she couldn't tell fortunes anymore, which meant Paul had just ruined their revenue stream. The owners accused him of disturbing the peace, and things went downhill fast. The magistrates tore the clothes off Paul and his traveling companion Silas, then had them beaten with rods and thrown in jail.

Their Philippi story had taken a turn.

But much like Meleeka's father, there in the depths of the prison, feet bound by stocks, the two men sang, and sang a lot. They prayed aloud. The other prisoners listened.

And then there was an earthquake, so great "the foundations of the prison were shaken. And immediately all the doors were opened, and everyone's bonds were unfastened" (v. 26). When the jailer woke up and saw the doors open, he assumed he had lost all the prisoners, and he drew his sword to kill himself. If men were beaten for disturbing the peace in Philippi, there wouldn't be much mercy for the guard who let a whole jail full of criminals go. But Paul shouted loudly from the inner prison, "Do not harm yourself, for we are all here" (v. 28).

The jailer trembled. He called for lights, and when he rushed in and saw them all, he fell down before Paul and Silas. "Sirs, what must I do to be saved?" (v. 30).

Jesus bent his path in the midst of Paul's persecution.

The officials let Paul and Silas go free that day. The jailer washed the men's wounds, and they baptized his whole family. The two said goodbye to Lydia—another life changed by their stay in Philippi—and then they moved on.

I have a feeling they would say *it was worth it all*.

WHEN PAIN AND JOY COEXIST

I'll never forget the day I got to meet Meleeka. It was before she fled to the United States, and it was in the middle of her father's second prison term. No one knew at that point when or if he would ever get out. They had hoped for some good news even that day and had gotten none. The law there wasn't necessarily bent in their favor.

When we arrived at her house, Meleeka and her mother and brothers sat on floor cushions in their living room and politely offered us tea and a seat to join them. We talked and laughed for a while, but it wasn't long before there were tears too. Before we left, Meleeka's mother began to pray long and loud, hands outstretched to heaven, the way someone does when her soul is crying out to God in pain. It was the pain of a wife missing her husband, the pain of a mother left with teenage boys who desperately needed a father's guidance. I felt as though we were intruding on an intimate moment between her and Jesus.

But as her cries echoed off the concrete walls, they settled in my heart. Her prayers turned to song, just like those of her husband, just like those of Paul and Silas. It was clear—Jesus owned the room. He owned her heart. He was her everything. She wanted her husband back—who wouldn't? But more than that, she wanted as many hearts as possible to know the Jesus she knew.

And in that moment, the veil between here and heaven got just a little thinner.

AS YOU PRAY

- Ask God to stay ever close to families like Meleeka's, families who suffer daily for their faith in Jesus Christ and their courage to share that faith with others.
- Ask Him to make the gospel go out in prisons and other places where believers are encountering nonbelievers who, like Lydia and the Philippian jailer, may have soft hearts to listen.
- Ask Him to give you a heart willing to go wherever He might lead, whatever the cost, so that others may know Him. It's not an easy prayer to pray, but He promises to never leave you, no matter what may come.

Day 25
He Urges Us to Go

"Are you sure?" the waitress asked again.

"Yes, I'm sure," John said.

"It's pretty spicy. Like really hot," she said.

"I know," John said with a smile. "It will be OK. I promise."

Our little group had just finished a day of standing on the street doing research in London, and we were recuperating with pizza. John had picked out one called "blazing hot pepper," or something like that, and the waitress didn't trust his judgment. He just smiled politely. What she didn't know—and what he told us after she walked away—was that he was from a remote village in India that was home to one of the hottest peppers in the world. Pizza Hut didn't have much of a chance of out-hotting him.

That story opened up a whole can of tales from John's part of the world. In his village, people believed that if you got bitten by a certain poisonous snake, the only thing that would counteract the poison was to eat the entire snake right then and there. When John was younger, he was bitten—and he did it.

"Did it work?"

"Well, something did," he said with a laugh. "I'm still here."

His village had a language all its own, and the woman he found to marry was an entire day's walk away—three different language groups lived in between his people and hers. So he would make the trek back and forth, and finally they married.

"How in the world did you get here?" someone asked.

He just smiled again as he ate his hot pepper pizza.

Somehow the gospel had made it to him, and somehow he had made it to London.

OVERWHELMING NEED

Earlier that day, as part of an ethnography class, we had been hanging out in the streets near London's Stratford station, the subway stop nearest Olympic Park. We'd been sent out to try to get a feel for what ethnicities lived in the area and who came and went from that station. The idea was to learn how to map a city so that church planters could know who was there and figure out the best ways to reach them.

From the first moment, I was overwhelmed.

Every minute, hundreds of people spilled out of the station doors and into the street, and it felt as though there were as many ethnicities as there were people. In some parts of the city, you might find more of a pocket of a certain people group or two or three, but here in Stratford it was like a saltshaker of skin colors, cultures, origins, and religions. As I stood in the street trying frantically to make notes, they spilled around me as though I were a tree standing dead center of a river.

So many people, just right here on this square of concrete. The act of trying to log them all made me realize just how many there were, and realizing how many there were made me wonder how many knew Jesus.

Not many, I guessed. And with that thought, for a moment, I was overcome. *How can we get hope to them? There are so many.*

Amy Carmichael, a missionary to India around the turn of the twentieth century, wrote once about a dream she had where she she stood on a cliff. An ocean of people walked toward her, spilling around her and stepping off the precipice behind her:

> **There was a woman with a baby in her arms and another little child holding on to her dress. She was on the very verge. Then I saw that she was blind. She lifted her foot for the next step . . . it trod air. She was over, and the children over with her.**

The cry as they fell was bloodcurdling, Carmichael wrote. And there were more and more and more, flowing over from every direction. She was glued to the spot and couldn't move, and she felt sheer agony as she watched and wondered why no one stopped them as they poured over the edge, falling into a gulf that "yawned like the mouth of hell."

Then she saw a few people sitting under some trees with their backs to the cliff. When she looked more closely, she realized they were making daisy chains.

Sometimes when a piercing shriek cut the quiet air and reached them, it disturbed them and they thought it a rather vulgar noise. And if one of their number started up and wanted to go and do something to help, then all the others would pull that one down. "Why should you get so excited about it? You must wait for a definite call to go! You haven't finished your daisy chain yet. It would be really selfish," they said, "to leave us to finish the work alone."

WHERE OUR RESPONSIBILITY MEETS GOD'S WORK

The need is unspeakably massive. The responsibility can be haunting.

But it's probably safe to say we're more in greater danger of feeling sluggish and apathetic than burdened to the point of breaking. That's what Carmichael's dream reminds us, and that's what Jesus reminds us when we read His words, "Look, I tell you, lift up your eyes, and see that the fields are white unto harvest. Already the one who reaps is receiving wages and gathering fruit for eternal life, so that sower and reaper may rejoice together" (John 4:35–36).

The need is great, and so is the responsibility.

But what Paul shows us in Athens is how our responsibility meets God's divine appointment. For the people in Athens who would hear Paul again and believe, God had been moving their lives for years toward this point so that they might find Him. When Paul walked out onto the proverbial cliff and yelled, "I know where you can find hope! *It's in Christ Jesus*," he was meeting them at the place for which God had been preparing them. Not everyone believed—some mocked, and the ocean of people continued to roar on. But some found Jesus that day (Acts 17:32–34).

It was God's doing. But it was Paul's responsibility to share.

Because he went, people like Dionysus the Areopagite and Damaris had their names added to the number of God's people. And because others go—people like Amy Carmichael—John and others in remote villages in India find Him. People in cities like London that are heaving with the masses find Him too.

We aren't waiting for a call—we love because He first loved us. And we chase others because He chases us.

AS YOU PRAY

- Ask God to help you love what He loves and chase what He chases. Ask Him to give you a sense of urgency for the eternal fate of the people around you every day, people He's pursuing, people bound for eternal suffering.
- Ask God to give His followers boldness to share their faith, regardless of the risk.
- Ask Him to soften hearts around the world and guide people down the road that leads to salvation.

Day 26
He Leads Us to Point Others to His Word

TODAY'S READING:
ACTS 17:10–15

Addisu's family told him he didn't deserve to live, and when he died, he wouldn't be buried. It's all because of what he did with his knife one day—and with his heart.

That day, Addisu had walked into the living room where his whole family was sitting. He slipped his finger under the black string tied around his neck and tugged on it gently, for the last time feeling its familiar pressure there. And then he lifted his knife and cut it off.

"In our country, a black string around the neck is a sign of being Orthodox, so I cut it off in front of my family as a symbol that I don't follow any religion—I follow Jesus Christ," he said. The persecution came immediately.

And when I met Addisu in Africa, I was confused at first as to why. His family was Orthodox, a religion full of crosses and paintings and things that seem centered on Jesus. It was weird to me that when their son dusted off the family Bible in the corner and decided to read it and do what it said, they told him he was a sellout, a rebel.

"In our culture, everything is done in community. If you go against the community, they may try to kill you. And my family, they would get kicked out of the funeral club because of what I did," Addisu said.

The funeral club?

"It's the club that you belong to so that when you die, someone will bury you," he said. "If you are kicked out of the funeral club, your body will just rot in your home." In their eyes, it doesn't get worse than that. And that's just one aspect of the community, a community that worships in churches with paintings of the crucifixion, the parables, the sacrifice of Christ.

But the community worships with other things too, like a gruesome story that got mixed in with the truth. According to Orthodox tradition there, a guy was plowing his field when some men showed up much as God showed up to speak with Abraham in Genesis. Except this time it was Satan, and Satan asked the guy to sacrifice his son and cook him. He did. And when he offered it to Satan, Satan told him to take the first bite. When he did, Satan revealed himself and that he had tricked the man, and the man went crazy. He went on a cannibalistic killing spree that took down his whole village.

As the story goes, when he was on his way to destroy another village, a man asked him to give him a cup of water in Jesus' name. He refused. So the guy asked for a cup of water in Mary's name, and the guy relented. So when it came time for the man to go to hell, Mary tipped the scales in his direction and let him go to heaven instead.

IT SATISFIES HUNGER WITH HOPE

It's bad enough there are scales involved in their view of what gets you to heaven—we know and are grateful that redemption is about Jesus' sacrifice for our sins, because our works would never measure in a way where we'd come out on top. Ever.

But the hero of the story is Mary—she's the one who brought the man redemption in this story. And as a friend said, this is when the gospel died in that part of Africa.

But God is still on the move among that people, through individuals like Addisu and believers who moved to Africa and planted their lives there so they could encourage Addisu to read the Bible in his house for himself and find out what it really said.

He did. They studied it together. And it wasn't long before he realized what it really said pointed straight to Jesus and a grace that made scales unnecessary.

"Every day I feel like I won the lottery," Addisu said. "That's the wealth I've been given in Jesus Christ. I get to watch people who have spiritual famine being satisfied with the Word of God."

DIGGING INTO THE TRUTH

Spiritual famine—that's what Paul found in Berea, the place he visited just before Athens. He found Jews still chained to their religion, trying to earn their own righteousness the same way he did in his old life. But he found that, like John, they received his message of hope "with all eagerness, examining the Scriptures daily to see if these things were so" (Acts 17:11). Paul said if they just dug into the pages of God's Word, they would see Jesus there, jumping out at them from every story, shouting at them from every prophecy. They would see Him as the Messiah worth following, the Christ who was worth cutting off their former allegiances and leaving everything behind.

They read daily—and they didn't just read, they examined. They asked questions. And many believed.

But the Jews in Thessalonica—the ones who accused Paul of turning the world upside down—heard he had moved on to Berea and that people were starting to believe what Paul preached. They had gotten him out of Thessalonica, but they really didn't want him turning Berea upside down either. So they came there too to stir up the crowds and get him driven out.

It wasn't an uncommon theme. He had been driven out before, and he would be driven out again. So would others. So had Jesus Himself.

For centuries, the darkness would try to squelch the light of the gospel—and for centuries, it would fail. In the years after Jesus' death, His disciples would be driven away, imprisoned, tortured, and killed for the Light. More than a millennium later, men like Martin Luther would sit in churches where they were taught that they had to pay for forgiveness by giving money to the church, and something would squirm in their souls until they went and read the Bible for themselves. They would see the truth, then fight for the true gospel, the one that had gotten distorted in their churches and communities.

And they would fight for the right of all people to read the Bible for themselves. Because that's where the truth is, and that's where we see God for who He really is. That's where chains fall off and hearts find freedom from the burden of heavy religion, the pressure to earn redemption, and the bondage of beliefs that offer false hope.

That's where we point people, just like believers in Africa pointed John, and just like Paul pointed the Jews in Berea. Go and read for yourself. Ask questions if you have them. Dig in until you know. You'll see. Jesus shouts at you from every page, and once you see Him for who He really is, you'll want to cut the cord from around your neck, even if that means you lose everything.

He's worth so much more.

And that light will never, ever be squelched.

AS YOU PRAY

- Ask God to draw you deeper into His Word so you can know the truth of who He is more and more all the time.
- Ask Him to bend the paths of people all over the world so that they encounter the Word of God.
- Ask Him to illuminate the words of Scripture in the hearts of people as they read and search for the truth.

Day 27
He Leads Us to Grieve for Others

TODAY'S READING:
ACTS 17:16

Prayer flags lined our way as we walked up to the temple, the small squares of fabric vivid against the foggy mountain backdrop. As our minds spun in silent prayer, we somberly greeted a man who was doing laps around the exterior of the building, his fingers brushing long rows of gold vertical cylinders with ornate inscriptions.

His job was to keep them spinning. As long as he did, he believed it meant prayers were rising to Buddha. We quietly watched. Other spinning prayer wheels were being powered by a nearby stream, completely detached from human involvement. Statues were scattered around the buildings—Buddha of course, but also Tara, a meditation deity, the "mother of liberation."

Liberation was all we wanted for them. Because as colorful as the flags were and as beautiful as the ornate gold, all we saw was one thing.

Idols.

Even up there in the thin, beautiful air of the Himalayas, it's as if oxygen felt heavy, as though we couldn't shake it off. Bondage was thick there. People had been spinning those wheels since just a few centuries after Paul spoke to the Athenians. That's a long, tragic lap for a people to make around a temple to a god who can't hear them. Be born, live in idolatry, die. Be born, live in idolatry, die. Spin, spin, spin.

And as we looked on it, our hearts were broken.

NOT THE WAY IT'S SUPPOSED TO BE

That's the way Paul felt the day he stood and surveyed Athens' idolatry, meaningless allegiances that flapped like prayer flags in the wind. The idols deeply troubled him. He knew what their worship signified. It wasn't that it was meaningless but also harmless; it was a straight and fast road to eternal suffering, a doorway to Satan himself. In his first letter to the church at Corinth, Paul said that what men sacrifice to idols "they offer to demons and not to God" (1 Corinthians 10:20).

If that was the case—and Paul believed it was—Satan had quite a hold on Athens. People there were in slavery to darkness and all that came with it, and as a result, they were shut off to what they really needed. As the Old Testament prophets said, to turn to idols is to destroy yourself (Hosea 8:4) and give up your chance for steadfast love (Jonah 2:8).

Even so, idols were everywhere.

Roman writer Petronius had joked that it was easier to find a god than a man in Athens around this time. He wasn't wrong. But Paul had a deep, gut-wrenching conviction that this wasn't the way it was supposed to be. So he backed that conviction with his passion, his time, his very life—and he spoke truth.

And even though he might have gotten discouraged at times, he said it was all worth it. He wrote to the believers in Thessalonica—people he had shared with just after his time in the Philippian jail—that "our coming to you was not in vain" (1 Thessalonians 2:1). They had turned away from their idols. They had run toward the freedom of Christ.

Paul knew their faith was real—he saw their joy in the midst of suffering. Others had noticed too—he told them so. "For not only has the word of the Lord sounded forth from you in Macedonia and Achaia, but your faith in God has gone forth everywhere" (1 Thessalonians 1:8).

They had seen Paul's example and followed it, just as Paul had seen Jesus' example and followed it. Love God. Love people as God does. Give your life for them. Shoulder hardship when necessary. That's what Paul did when he saw the Thessalonians in bondage to idols. "We were ready to share with you not only the gospel of God but also our own selves" (1 Thessalonians 2:8).

He did this over and over and over again, in different places. He found he couldn't stop as long as God kept sending him—and as long as he could still see their idols.

That's the way my friends in the Himalayas felt about the people there, the ones spinning the prayer wheels. Their hearts were broken over the people's bondage, and they were ready to endure suffering—altitude sickness, homesickness, rejection, and whatever else might come—to take the gospel to them. Some of the places are hard to get to. Sometimes they hike for days to get to these places, and when they do, the vast majority of the people aren't interested in what they have to say.

But one friend said that after seeing their idols, he just couldn't stop.

"I'm up there on the mountain, wearing six jackets and three gloves and five socks, and I really just kind of want to sit in a bed," he said. "But then you think about those people. If we turn around, who is going to come next? I mean, how many people have turned around? There's no excuse for turning back. We keep going."

He holds his hiking poles up in the shape of a cross and tells the story of Jesus, over and over. Occasionally someone says, "We will hear you again about this."

And occasionally someone believes.

THE CRY OF BLOOD

Once you let the sound of their hopelessness, the futility of their worship, seep into your soul, it's haunting in a way you can't shake—a way that drives you forward. Amy Carmichael said that in her dream, the people who were ignoring the masses began to sing a hymn, but "through the hymn came another sound like the pain of a million broken hearts rung out in one full drop, one sob. And a horror of great darkness was upon me, for I knew what it was—the Cry of Blood."

It was the sound of blood spilled, blood that could've been saved had somebody gone. It was followed by the sound of God's voice holding people responsible—the people who could see the cliff and didn't move to go save those who were spilling over to their death.

"What does it matter, after all? It has gone on for years; it will go on for years. Why make such a fuss about it?" Carmichael asked. "God forgive us! God arouse us! Shame us out of our callousness! Shame us out of our sin!"

God, help us say what my friend in the Himalayas says. *There's no excuse for turning back. We keep going.*

Let's not let another day pass when we drown out their cries. Let's not let another week pass when we don't discipline ourselves to dig deep in the Word, for our own sake and for the sake of others.

And let's not let a lifetime pass in which we occasionally look in the direction of the cliff, get disturbed for a moment, and then turn back to our normal, peaceful lives. Too many idols scream Satan's plans for premeditated murder of souls. Too many people can't see that they're being led to the slaughter. Too much is at stake.

And God puts the message in our mouths and says *go*.

AS YOU PRAY

- Ask God to break your heart for the lost, to love them as He does, to stop at nothing to see them rescued from death.
- Ask Him to give more and more believers a sense of urgency, that they might intentionally go to plant their lives in places where people have never heard—or simply be aware of the lost around them every single day, right where they live.
- Ask God to give believers restlessness and courage to act on that conviction as Paul did.

Day 28
He Calls Us to
Difficult Places

TODAY'S READING:
ACTS 17:32—18:11

As the plane backed away from the gate, I sank down into the seat, allowing myself to decompress. I looked out the window, tracing the city with my eyes.

That out there. That's a hard place. A hard place to live, and a hard place to share Jesus.

My friends who had planted their lives in that North African country are heroes to me, but they battle exhaustion—and rightly so. Inside the confines of their houses, they can breathe, listen to music, make enchiladas, and hear themselves think. But when they walk outside, they instantly give up their rights to peace. For the women, that means catcalls, whistles, and aggressive comments from the moment they walk out the door until the moment they get back home. It's not dangerous usually, but it does turn an afternoon walk to the grocery store into a few verbal battles, a good bit of yelling, and maybe even getting touched. The culture is one of shame, but the shame doesn't usually come from people feeling bad for what they do—it comes from being yelled at until you stop whatever it is you're doing.

Over and over and over.

Daily.

Having to deal with that can wear you down—and that's just what it's like to walk down the street. Try sharing Christ, and it gets even tougher. People are resistant, hostile even. And for someone there to consider following Christ means considering mockery, rejection, even death.

So results are rare. And harassment is constant. It's tiring.

To keep pressing on takes superhuman strength.

THE STRENGTH TO CARRY ON

It's possible that's where Paul was toward the end of his time in Athens—tired. He had already been run out of Thessalonica and Berea, beaten, stoned, and put in prison, and now in Athens, his message was mocked. Historically, people who were given the floor to address the Areopagus got six minutes to share whatever it is they had to say, and if you timed Paul's speech, he might have gotten through only about a minute's worth before the mockery cut him off.

Some wanted to hear more. Some decided to believe.

But there was likely no big church that got started in Athens because of that day at the Areopagus—there were no letters from Paul to the Athenians as there were to the Corinthians, the Philippians, or the Ephesians. The amount of hardship compared to the measurable results might have seemed overwhelming. It's possible he was starting to get discouraged as he made his way to Corinth in Acts 18:1, because God showed up in a vision there and said, "Do not be afraid, but go on speaking and do not be silent, for I am with you, and no one will attack you to harm you, for I have many in this city who are my people" (v. 10).

It didn't mean Paul wouldn't still face difficult things—the Jews attacked him here too and brought him to court. But God was with him, as He had said, and Paul trusted Him. And with that, he had the strength to keep going.

IN IT FOR THE LONG HAUL

I saw a similar picture in the life of one of my friends there in that hard country—a woman who had moved from the United States with her husband and small children and planted her family there years ago. After years of praying, sharing truth, and shouldering hard moments, she finally saw a twenty-something girl come to Jesus—and then win her entire circle of friends to faith in Him.

I saw that same faith in the life of another couple I met—a young family who had moved to Southeast Asia to find ways to hike into the mountains and locate people groups who were hard to access. One of the groups they worked with was a fourteen-day journey away by four-wheel drive and high-altitude hiking. Just to walk to the village, snap a picture, and turn around and walk back took nearly a month. Stay in the village for any length of time to build relationships, and it would take much longer.

Not only that—the people were resistant to the gospel. Much like Addisu in Africa, their community would shun them if they believed. It often took a long time to build relationships and even have the opportunity to share, and it often took even longer for them to believe once they heard.

"We're always hopeful for miracles, but we're in it for the long haul," my friend there said. "We came knowing it might take a lot of hard years before we saw anyone believe."

THE "YES" OF OUR WHOLE HEART

I'd love to be like one of them. They're my heroes—people who have built quiet, extraordinary, faith-filled lives in these countries in order to break through the hopelessness and tell people of the love, freedom, and peace they can find in Jesus Christ. And not the leisurely, catcall-free walk to the grocery store kind of peace. The inner peace that will last for eternity.

But as I left that hard country and sank deeply into the window seat on the plane, I let myself be honest. I relished the peace. I thought of the green hills of England, where I lived at the time. I thought about my local Starbucks and the men I passed on the street who would smile kindly and walk on. And I realized there's a fine line between gratitude and entitlement, and once again, my heart had jumped so far over it that the line had retreated faster than a British summer.

I felt a check in my heart that made me realize, once again, He didn't have all of me.

Not all of us end up in Northern Africa or Southeast Asia. But it's possible that more of us should, and that's what I was wrestling with that day on the plane—putting my "yes" back on the table with God, whatever that meant, whatever things I might have to give up. It wasn't about me. It was about His glory in the nations and how everything else should slip through my fingers like desert sand so I could grab hold of Him and take Him to others. It's about knowing Him and making Him known to every person who's never known the name of Jesus, to everyone in the world.

Sometimes He has us in a place that has green grass, a place where trips to the grocery store are peaceful. When He does, there's a purpose. When He has me there, I want to make sure I use that season to enjoy Him and show Him to others right where I am.

But I should always have my everything on the table, asking Him what He wants for today, for tomorrow, for the future. I should always be willing to go.

Someone brought hope to me and to you when we didn't even know what we were missing, when we didn't see our chains.

Who will take it to them?

AS YOU PRAY

- Tell God that you love Him more than the things that are most important to you in your life—enough to leave them behind if He asked. If you find that hard to do but really mean it, then ask Him to teach your heart how to love Him above everything else.
- Ask God to call laborers to go into the harvest—a harvest that's ready and waiting.
- Ask Him if the person He would like to send is you.

Day 29
He Brings Freedom

The round beams from the headlamps chased each other up the dim stairwells, and we followed them.

I ran my fingers along the dusty walls of the corridors. Not much traffic passes this way. Even in the dark, that much was clear. The beams kept running on ahead of us, bouncing the way they do when they're attached to the foreheads of preschool boys.

And suddenly the darkness broke above us by way of a creaky metal door, and we were set free.

Up here on the roof, the breeze skirted the flat, circular space, ruffling the little boys' hair around the straps of their headlamps. The concrete walls of the rooftop curved up at the sides like the lip of a plate, stopping at just about eye level so you could peer down over them at the crush of high-rise apartment complexes below. It was like being in a fishbowl, a big concrete one, suspended dozens of stories above the ground. Except that in this fishbowl we could see out and no one else could see in.

"We had a friend who would climb up to the roof sometimes just because it was the only place he could go where no one could see him," my friend Sarah said with a laugh. She comes up here for the same reason—to let the blond-headed boys run around free all by themselves under a sky zigzagged with clotheslines. As the daylight faded, the sunbaked concrete roof cooled and the megacity breeze hit us all like sea air on a sunburn.

It felt amazing. We breathed. It was different up here.

Sarah said they once counted the windows they could see from their living room and estimated that maybe half a million people lived *just in their line of sight from one window.*

From up there, we had a 360-degree view of high-rise after high-rise stacked on top of each other. Looking down over the wall was like peering into giant boxes packed to the gills with the trappings of life—school and jobs and family and cooking dinner. Windows and windows and windows into millions of lives, all living and breathing and striving for something. It's a billion-ton train, one big collective worldwide breath we're breathing, crushed up against neighbors and friends and family, eyes forward, not up.

As individualistic as we like to think we are, we know it's true. And here from the roof, it shows. People for miles and miles, doing the same thing, all piled on top of each other, every day. Like the people of Athens, worldwide humanity as a whole is living, breathing, chasing dreams and worshipping things that don't matter. They're building altars to the things the culture says bring happiness, vindicate your soul, or bring good karma. Or maybe all those people are simply too distracted to think about it at all—they're just raising families and chasing careers and never looking up, numbing the gnawing feeling, doing laundry and going to bed and waking up and doing it all over again until they die.

It takes a lot to wreck something like that. It takes a lot to even realize that it can be wrecked.

WHEN LIFE GETS REBUILT

As I stood on the roof, eyes scanning the tiny windows, the dusk breeze filling my lungs, I thought about what it means to live for a God we can't see when all we know is to live like everyone we see. What does it mean to follow Him radically when it makes no sense in the framework of what we know of the world?

What does it mean for us to really believe that God can pluck us from a sea of billions and give us freedom?

I took a long, deep breath. *It wrecks us*, I thought. *That's all it can do. There's no alternative.*

A few days later, I sat on the living room floor next to someone who lived behind one of those tiny windows. She said her life used to rise and fall on the wind of that worldwide breath. Plans. Goals. Back then, she was doing OK. She wasn't really interested in being set free from the tidal pull of the masses. She didn't see a reason to want something different. She didn't know what freedom felt like in her lungs.

"But now I know," she said with a big smile. "I tell my friends I don't know how to explain it to them . . . I don't know how to explain what it feels like. Jesus wrecks your life, everything you think you know. Everything you've learned about how to live, He tears it all down. And then He rebuilds it."

WE RUN AND KEEP RUNNING

The night we stood on the roof, as I watched the boys run and tumble, I thought about freedom. I thought about how with faith we can reach up and grasp it, faith tinier than a mustard seed, faith that can move mountains. Faith that can overturn high-rise apartments full of the clutter of our lives. Faith that is willing to trade everything earthly for two lungs full of the air up here, two lungs full of the kind of freedom that can turn our lives absolutely upside down. It's the kind of freedom found in the resurrected Christ that Paul preached, the One who conquered death, the One who offered that life to us if we would just believe and break the cycle and give Him everything.

I thought about the corridor we used to get up to the roof. *Few find it. But that doesn't mean it's not there. And that doesn't mean the freedom at the end isn't real.*

It takes adult discipline. It takes childlike abandon. We have to walk away from the clutter—all of it. We have to get off the couch, strap on that light, and make that climb to ever taste it for ourselves. We dive into who God is in His Word, begging Him to show us Himself at any cost, because the payoff is worth it. We wake up early. We keep His name on our lips and our hearts. We run like kids aching to be set free. We ask for it. We strive for it. He hears.

It's hard to explain, but when that door cracks open and we truly believe, one thing's for sure.

It's worth that climb.

AS YOU PRAY

- Ask God to give you an intensified focus on the things that last—knowing God, loving people, and helping others find freedom in Christ.
- Ask Him to burden your heart for the millions upon millions of people around the world who live and die without knowing Jesus.
- Ask Him to draw people all over the world into places where they can hear the gospel and find Him.

Day 30
He Finishes What He Starts

TODAY'S READING:
1 CORINTHIANS 15:58

I've never been to the Areopagus, but my friend Amy says the path there is well worn. The marble steps leading up to the rock dip and sag in the middle, rubbed slippery and smooth by the steps of people walking over and over them for years—years that slowly slipped into millennia.

It's amazing how the hearts of people can turn into deeply rutted roads—and thousands upon thousands follow right in that well-beaten path. I think of people gathering on top of the Areopagus, and I think of them ascending the nearby Parthenon to worship their gods, and I get the image in my head all over again of the ocean of people going over the cliff in Amy Carmichael's dream, falling into a tormented eternity.

The task seems too daunting at times.

But then I remember something else. It may be narrow, but there's something else well worn—the path to Jesus. Those steps have been washed in love and sacrifice, etched into the path ahead of us by the footsteps of the faithful. Abraham, who left his homeland because God told him to follow Him. Noah, who, even though it didn't make sense to him, built a boat because he feared God, and God told him to do it. Peter, who asked Jesus, "Lord, to whom would we go?" Because of their faithfulness, two thousand years later we have the gospel.

And we continue to pass it on, our hearts making a road for others to follow.

With that cloud of witnesses in mind, we're encouraged to lay aside every weight and run as though we're running for the greatest prize we could ever be offered. We're urged to throw down the sin that clings so closely. And we're encouraged to persevere, always "looking to Jesus, the founder and perfecter of our faith, who for the joy that was set before him endured the cross, despising the shame, and is seated at the right hand of the throne of God" (Hebrews 12:2).

We're in good company. We know people have wandered this road before us, strangers and aliens on the earth, following Jesus and sharing Him with others no matter the cost. We know God has called out some from every nation, tribe, people, and language, just as He did in Athens. That includes some from the people in Nepal who are a fourteen-day journey away from my friends. That includes Syrians like the ones who met Maheer in their refugee camp tent.

We know it includes them because the Apostle John gives us a picture of what that's going to look like one day after this life is over:

After this I looked, and behold, a great multitude that no one could number, from every nation, from all tribes and peoples and languages, standing before the throne and before the Lamb, clothed in white robes, with palm branches in their hands, and crying out with a loud voice, "Salvation belongs to our God who sits on the throne, and to the Lamb!"
—Revelation 7:9–10

His Word is sure. His character is worthy of the eternal praise of every nation. We will end up in a place with people won from every language, tribe and tongue.

And with that confidence, we keep chasing God and chasing people.

SHE FELT FOR HIM AND FOUND HIM

It was months after the oak tree fell through Evelyn's new house when she realized it—"I'm different from what I was." After the tree changed her path and she moved to another city, she ended up in a job with someone who looked really different from anyone she had ever seen. Her coworker was free—really free. It was because of Jesus. And it showed. "It was when I got to know her that I knew I wanted to have what she had," Evelyn said. "It was so different."

And so, like the people in Berea, Evelyn began to try to figure out what it was really all about. She started to read the Bible for herself, cover to cover, learning its whole story. She became passionate about the God of the Bible, the One who held her whole life, the One who began to pull everything together in a way that made the world make sense. She got that there was suffering, sure—but life had momentum, purpose, drive. Jesus was worth everything. His story, from creation to redemption to His promised return, had captured her.

And she says now that, no question, she's grateful for that tree.

OUR PART OF THE BEST STORY

Ever since God bent your path with an oak tree moment, or several oak tree moments, He's had a path for you to walk—a pursuit of Him and others modeled after His own unshakable pursuit of us. You love because He first loved you. You chase because He first chased you.

And because of Christ's victory over death, we know it's all infused with eternal purpose. Paul reminds us of that in 1 Corinthians 15:58 (CEV)—"My dear friends, stand firm and don't be shaken. Always keep busy working for the Lord. You know that everything you do for him is worthwhile." Our labor here is the work of relentlessly putting the gospel before those who haven't yet heard and accepted it.

God pursued us in Christ. In response, we pursue Him back. And in that life and hope, we go to others, knowing that even if the gospel is mocked by some, God is still bringing people to Himself. He's still adding to the throng of all peoples that will be around His throne. And He's patient toward us, not wanting any to perish but allowing time for more to repent (2 Peter 3:9).

Our labor is not in vain.

So, friends, run with abandon. Labor with passion. Throw off the things that weigh you down and set your affections on the one true God.

You have nothing to lose and everything to gain.

AS YOU PRAY

- Ask God to help you see your life as part of His story, with your path bent for His purposes so you can know Him better and bring others to know Him.
- Ask Him once again to reveal places in your heart and life where He might not have all of you.
- Ask Him to guide you to the places and the people you need to encounter today . . . then again tomorrow, the next day, and the rest of your life.

If you enjoyed this book, will you consider sharing the message with others?

Let us know your thoughts at info@newhopepublishers.com. You can also let the author know by visiting or sharing a photo of the cover on our social media pages or leaving a review at a retailer's site. All of it helps us get the message out!
Twitter.com/NewHopeBooks
Facebook.com/NewHopePublishers
Instagram.com/NewHopePublishers

New Hope® Publishers is an imprint of Iron Stream Media, which derives its name from Proverbs 27:17,
"As iron sharpens iron, so one person sharpens another."

For more information on ISM and New Hope Publishers, please visit
IronStreamMedia.com
NewHopePublishers.com

This sharpening describes the process of discipleship, one to another. With this in mind, Iron Stream Media provides a variety of solutions for churches, missionaries, and nonprofits ranging from in-depth Bible study curriculum and Christian book publishing to custom publishing and consultative services. Through the popular Life Bible Study and Student Life Bible Study brands, ISM provides web-based full-year and short-term Bible study teaching plans as well as printed devotionals, Bibles, and discipleship curriculum.